SAVED AND KEPT

SAVED AND KEPT

COUNSELS TO YOUNG BELIEVERS

BY THE REV.

F. B. MEYER

OF CHRIST CHURCH, WESTMINSTER BRIDGE ROAD
LONDON

WIPF & STOCK · Eugene, Oregon

Wipf and Stock Publishers
199 W 8th Ave, Suite 3
Eugene, OR 97401

Saved and Kept
Counsels to Young Believers
By Meyer, F.B.
ISBN 13: 978-1-5326-1749-2
Publication date 1/30/2017
Previously published by
Fleming H. Revell, Co., 1897

CONTENTS

		PAGE
PREFACE		5
I.	A Form of Dedication	7
II.	The Marks of Genuine Faith	13
III.	"Wilt Thou be Made Whole?"	19
IV.	"When I had Ceased from my Struggles"	26
V.	"Bid Me Come!"	32
VI.	Not "Attain," but "Obtain"	39
VII.	At the Gate of the Will	43
VIII.	The Control of our Thoughts	49
IX.	Not Joy, but Christ	55
X.	The Hour of Temptation	60
XI.	The Conqueror from Edom	67
XII.	Our Ideals	74
XIII.	How to Receive	80

CONTENTS

		PAGE
XIV. Our Equableness	. . .	87
XV. Unspotted	. . .	94
XVI. Use your Senses	. . .	101
XVII. The Light of that Day	.	108
XVIII. The Secret of Continuance	.	115
XIX. One of God's "Noes"	.	122
XX. Forgetting	. . .	129
XXI. Stay where You Are	.	135
XXII. What have You to Give?	.	141
XXIII. The Presence of God	.	147

PREFACE

It is my fiftieth birthday. Goodness and mercy have followed me all the days of my life, and I trust I have entered the house of the Lord to stay there forever.

But the review of the past brings back to memory the recollection of so many turned lessons, so much failure and sin, that one would despair were it not for the blood that cleanseth from all sin.

That past may be forgiven, but it cannot be undone; and the only way to utilize it is to derive lessons and warnings for the benefit of those that are following after. And so these words have been written, largely for my young sisters and brothers on each side of the Atlantic, and also for all who desire to know the secret of being SAVED AND KEPT.

F. B. MEYER.

CHRIST CHURCH,
WESTMINSTER BRIDGE ROAD,
April 8, 1897.

SAVED AND KEPT

I

A FORM OF DEDICATION

"I will pay my vows unto the Lord."—Ps. CXVI. 16–18.

THIS form of dedication is offered to be used by each alone, in some quiet place, as a suggestion of some deeper acts.

I come to Thee, most blessed Lord, to renew my vows. My soul lies low in penitence before Thee, as I recall all Thy patience and loving-kindness, Thy forbearance and tender pity, toward one of the most unworthy of Thy followers. I have so often failed Thee and brought shame upon Thy name; I have disappointed Thee, when I might have given Thee pleasure; I have thwarted Thee, when I might have yielded to Thy holy purpose. My only plea is Thy most precious blood. Thou hast magnified Thy mercy in saving me at all; now magnify Thy grace in forgiving and restoring my soul. Let me now stand again in Thy holy presence and speak with Thee face to face.

"Nothing between, Lord, nothing between."

From this moment I solemnly, and by Thy grace, renounce and put away the evil things which have usurped an unholy supremacy with me — the companionships that lower the temperature of my inner life; the books and amusements which have cast a shadow on my hours of fellowship; the sin which so easily besets me; the soft yielding to sloth which has robbed me of so many seasons of hallowed communion; the desire to please men rather than Thee, and to succeed in this world rather than to be a humble servant in Thy glorious household. All these I hereby steadfastly renounce and forsake. Other lords have had dominion over me, but henceforth by Thee only will I make mention of Thy name. Especially do I steadfastly resolve by Thy grace to renounce the devil and all his works; the world and all its vanity; the flesh and all its selfish and sinful desires, so that I may not follow or be led by them. In myself I cannot keep these resolutions — my will is like a bruised reed, my desires like smoking flax; but oh, keep me true! Thou hast kept my soul from death;

wilt Thou not also keep my feet from falling, that I may walk before the Lord in the light of the living? Thou art able to keep me from stumbling and present me faultless before the presence of Thy glory with exceeding joy; into Thy hands I commend my spirit; and I am persuaded that Thou dost accept and wilt keep what I commit to Thee against that day.

And now, Lord, I yield myself to Thee,— spirit, soul, and body,— that as these were once filled and used by the Spirit of Evil, they may henceforth be filled and used by Thy Holy Spirit, who is one with Thee and the Father in the mystery of the Holy Trinity. Never again, by Thy dear help, shall sin reign in my mortal body, that I should obey the lusts thereof. It may tempt me by its suggestions; but it shall not reign, since I desire to present myself unto God as one alive from the dead, and my members as instruments of righteousness unto God.

In my inner life I desire to be kept absolutely pure and lovely. O Holy and Spotless One, be in me the crystal fountain of purity! O Lamb of God, be in me the source of absolute meekness and humility! O Lover of men, be in me a fire of unwaning, all-subduing tenderness! Make me instantly sensitive to the least taint of impurity and uncharity. Before ever the suggestion has assumed a tangible shape, may I detect it and shelter in Thee.

In my home life may I be made a blessing: its sunbeam when the days are dark; its inspiration when the days are sad and hopeless; its tender comfort when the days are full of pain and tears. Always thinking of others before myself; never imposing my private sorrows or moods; ever with the girt loin and the lighted torch; washing my face, and anointing my head, and confiding my griefs to Thee only, that I may ever have

> "A heart at leisure from itself,
> To soothe and sympathize."

In my religious life may the neglect of prayer and Thy Holy Word be things of the past. Wake me morning by morning to hear as a disciple. Enable me to spring up at Thy call, and, like all Thy true servants, to rise up early in the morning to gather the manna ere the dew be gone from it. May my fellowship with Thee be unbroken through the day, that I may often look up into Thy face, even if I have not time to speak. Draw me, and I will run after Thee.

> "Each moment call from earth away
> My soul, that only waits Thy call."

In my daily calling make me diligent in business, fervent in spirit, serving the Lord.

May I do my work, not for the wages I may get, nor to secure an advance, but so as to please Thee. May it be the one object of my daily striving to do all to the glory of God—not with eye-service, as pleasing men, but in singleness of heart, fearing the Lord, doing the will of God as it is indicated in the circumstances of my life, and looking for my reward from Thy hand, O divine Master!

In my use of money I would not be anxious about the future, nor hoard up and keep for myself of that which Thou hast given me; I want to be Thy very slave, counting myself and all I have as Thy purchased property, and using all things as Thy representative and steward.

In my use of time and health and all the opportunities of life I desire to act with reverent care, redeeming the time, buying up each opportunity, conserving my body as the pure temple of the Holy Ghost, so partaking of recreation, food, natural scenery, travel, and all lawful pastimes, that I may the better serve Thy purpose in my creation and redemption. Show me what my talents are which Thou hast intrusted to me, and help me to make the two four and the five ten.

Now bless me, even me, O Lord. I am Thine; Thy Father gave me to Thee before the world was made; Thou didst purchase me for Thyself by Thy most precious blood;

Thou hast begun a good work within me by Thy Holy Spirit ; and now afresh take me to Thine heart and seal me with Thy Spirit. May He enlighten, comfort, and sanctify me, teaching me to pray, and opening the eyes of my heart that I may know Thee and the power of Thy resurrection, that as Thou hast ascended into the heavens, so I may also in heart and mind thither ascend, and with Thee continually dwell, who livest and reignest with the Father and the Holy Spirit, one God, world without end. Amen.

II

THE MARKS OF GENUINE FAITH

"He that believeth on the Son hath everlasting life."—JOHN III. 36.

It is very necessary sometimes to ask, especially at the beginning of our Christian life, if we are really right—there are so many counterfeits in the world and the church, and when once we have received the stamp and imprimatur of some Christian body we are apt to trust it as decisive in all after time, so that when appeals are addressed to the unconverted and halting, we at once pass them off to others, feeling sure that they cannot apply to ourselves. How often do souls sit in a very shower of gospel blessing, covered by the umbrella of having been accepted by a church, or of the approval of the leaders of a Christian Endeavor Society, passing away to others what was meant for, and needed by, themselves! When once unconverted persons become dubbed as Christians, it is the hardest matter possible to convince them of their need of the gospel. Again, I say, it is most necessary to be quite sure that we are really right.

There was a great ado recently because foreign and inferior goods were being imported into England and stamped with the mark of the Sheffield manufacturers. They went out into all the world as English make, when, in point of fact, they were the poorest German. People did not think of questioning the genuineness of the articles, because they were assured by the Sheffield stamp. After a time had passed we can almost imagine the articles themselves, thus labeled, beginning to fancy that they were genuine, and if even their right to be accounted so were challenged by the other cutlery amid which they lay, they would haughtily decline to enter into the discussion, content to quote the fact of having been properly stamped. "Do you question my right to call myself a Sheffield blade, when I have the Sheffield stamp so clearly indented?" So men ignore your appeals if once they have been accounted truly regenerate by the recognized leaders of some Christian society.

The necessity for close self-scrutiny is the more obvious when we come face to face with the searching words of the apostle James. We have been wont to insist on faith as the essential of salvation; but he tells us that there are two kinds of faith, and it may be that, after all, we have the wrong one. It is not sufficient to say we have faith; we must be sure that it is *saving* faith, which links the soul with the Saviour.

True faith has Christ for its object. Many times the question is put by the inquirer, "Have I the right kind of faith?" To this there is only one answer: "When the soul moves toward Christ as its Saviour, when it turns even from the facts of His life and work to Himself, it is the faith of God's elect, which He hath Himself breathed into the soul." All faith that has Christ for its object is the right kind of faith. It may bring no conscious rapture; it may be weak as the woman's touch on His garment hem; it may be small and insignificant as a grain of mustard-seed; it may be despairful as Peter's cry, "Lord, save, or I perish!" But if its deepest yearning is Christ, Christ, Christ, it is the tiny thread which will bring the lost one through the subterranean passages, in which it had surrendered itself as lost, into the light of life.

True faith is trust. "Trust" is a more personal word than "faith." We *believe* the record of history; we have *faith* in our friend's word of honor; but we TRUST the one we love. In the beginning of Christian life, while yet the soul is looking around for help, it deals specially with statements about Christ, and perhaps with His precious promises; but afterward it closes in with Christ Himself, and from that moment it rests, not on the deed, but on the Doer; not on the word, but on Him who uttered it; not on the atonement, but on Him who died; not on the resurrection, but on Him who rose; not on the intercession, but on Him who ever liveth to make it.

True faith reckons on God's faith. Spurious faith tries to confirm itself by culling the favorable reports that others give it, or by considering the amount of religiousness with which it is accompanied. It is always eager to maintain a certain frame or atmosphere of this same religiousness, in order to assure itself that it is not a counterfeit. But a true faith looks away from all such considerations to God, and reckons that He is true; that He cannot disavow His offspring; that He cannot fail the soul He has attracted to Himself; that He must meet it when it is a great way off, and spread the feast. There is no better way of nurturing faith than by looking away from it to its object. When you believe not, He remaineth faithful. Give up estimating the force of your faith, or searching for the roots of it, or analyzing its component parts. Begin to consider the impossibility of God denying Himself, and as you do so the true faith will stir within you; by considering God's faith, your faith will grow strong to remove mountains.

The true faith is followed by penitence. Repentance and penitence differ vastly. Repentance precedes and accompanies faith; penitence follows it. Repentance has its seat in the will; penitence in the emotions. Repentance is the forsaking of sin; penitence the abhorring and grieving for it. Repentance may therefore take place once for all, as we turn from our evil life to God; penitence runs parallel with all Christian experience. The nearer we come to Christ the more we grieve for the sorrow we have given Him. When the woman reached the feet of Christ, and knew herself forgiven, she covered them with tears and kisses. The faith which is dry-eyed is a very doubtful sort.

True faith detaches from the world and sin in proportion as it attaches to Christ. It clings to Him, and is so taken up with His love and beauty that it loses a taste for what had before filled its horizon and had seemed altogether essential to its existence. Its treasure is in heaven, and its heart is there also.

True faith bears fruit. We have said it is the link between Christ and the soul through which the living energy of Christ pours into us, as the sap from the root to the cluster of ruddy grapes swelling on the branch. It is impossible to be in true union with Christ without feeling the pulse of His glorious life, and where it enters like a tidal river it can have but one result—it must manifest itself in fruit. When there is no fruit either the channel is grievously choked or has never been truly formed.

It is well, therefore, now and then, to take the enumeration of fruit given in Galatians v., and to stay prayerfully over each grace, questioning whether it is present, and, being present, if it is becoming more marked in our experience. Do not trouble about the roots; consider the fruit. Examine yourselves whether ye be in the faith.

If you have not faith, or fear that your faith is wrong, do not despair or give way to introspection. Look away to Jesus. Open your heart that God may put into it the gift of the true faith. Believe He does so at the moment of your asking. Go forth and live in the power of that belief. Reckon that God is true. Feed your faith on its native bread—the Word of God. Nourish it by climbing to the heights of communion, where it may breathe its native air.

III

"WILT THOU BE MADE WHOLE?"

JOHN v. 6.

IN one of the five porches of the Pool of Siloam, for thirty-eight years, this man had lain until hope had died out. He had made so many ineffectual attempts to reach the troubled water when it was impregnated with healing virtue! Time after time—so often that he had long lost count—he had dragged himself almost to the edge, but there was always some one else, either nimbler of limb, or better provided with a little band of helpers, whose love had made them dexterous. Always some other man stepped down before him! Always the hope was deferred! So the eyes grew weary of watching for the mysterious motion of the water, and even if healing should come, life was too far gone to make it specially valuable. To him Christ came with the appeal, "Wilt thou be made whole?" (John v. 6.)

He was suffering from paralysis, which had affected his motor nerves. He knew exactly what he wanted to do, and the limbs with which to do it; his brain was perfectly able to issue its commands, but there was no power of transmitting the nervous energy so as to react upon the muscles and through them on the limbs. To know how to do was present with him; but how to perform that which was good he found not. He often lay and pondered with himself some swifter means of reaching the pool; but when the moment arrived for executing his purpose the deep-seated paralysis put an arrest on his plan.

We all suffer more or less from a similar paralysis. Have you never sat in a public conveyance, and desired to speak to some lonely girl or lad, and felt the message petrified upon your lips? That is the paralysis of speech. Have you never felt that you ought to give to some crying case of need, but the opportunity has passed and the unfortunate drifted away into the dark? That is the paralysis of benevolence. Have you never felt the conception of an unselfish act beckoning you to a life or an act of self-giving, but the vision has died away, leaving you wrapped up in the pursuit of your own aims and delights? That is the paralysis of well-doing. "Withered" is a very accurate epithet

"WILT THOU BE MADE WHOLE?"

for much of our life. The sensory nerves convey the impressions from without, but the motor nerves of the moral nature fail to obey the promptings of the will. To us, too, Jesus says, "Wilt thou be made whole?"

Whole! That would mean that the life should obey the noblest ideas that pass across our inner vision; that would mean that there should be no break between the divine inspirations and our fulfilment; that would mean that when God called us by name we should, like Abraham, answer, "Here am I!" and start early in the morning, though it were to the mountain of sacrifice. Whole! That means the single eye, perfected consecration, the response to the cup and cross without murmuring or complaint.

The primary condition of being made whole is in the will. *Wilt* thou be made whole? Granted that the will has become enfeebled by constantly yielding its scepter to passion, — like one of the early English kings, a mere puppet in the hands of strong barons, — yet Christ must know that its choice is on His side before He will set on foot the health-giving processes. He is prepared to be told that the will is vacillating and weak. This is no disappointment. He is well able to work in us to will and to do, when once the will has made its appeal to Him. The governor of a province might be overpowered by a revolt and yet be true in his allegiance to his suzerain.

Wilt thou, young soul, be made whole? You have been double-minded; will you have the single eye? You have been double-hearted; will you have the single purpose? You have been infirm in purpose, cowardly in confession, paralyzed in action; do you choose at whatever cost to be made whole, as those angels that excel in strength and do His commandments, hearkening unto the voice of His word? Are you willing to be made whole—though it should involve you in obloquy and scorn; though it mean the loss of companionships that have been as the apple of your eye, and the forsaking of those scenes which are familiar as the porch where this man had sheltered for thirty-eight years? Tell the Saviour so! Discover the one point in your character in which this moral paralysis has worked most disastrously. Tell Christ you are eager to be made whole just there; and He who knows the length of time that you have been in this evil case will not fail to heal and make you every whit whole.

The second step is to claim His healing virtue. That man's faith, opened by the question of Christ, received from Him healing virtue. He did not supplicate, or agonize, or even pray. He just looked, received, and was whole. You do not need strong faith

"WILT THOU BE MADE WHOLE?" 23

for this, but Christ. The whole ocean may flow through a narrow aperture if you will give it time enough. In fact, the weaker your faith is the better will be your chance with Christ. Whom would you save first in a wreck—the man in whom life is strong, or the child whose tiny hand is waxing weary? Surely the latter. Weakness has a prior claim than strength. I have known a strong man, the Samson of the country-side, bend to the earth before the thin arms of his sickly child stretched out toward him. He would pass by the healthy lads and girls of the family to give himself to the little helpless cripple. Suppose a fire were to break out in that man's cottage; would he not save that withered nursling before the children who were well able to help themselves? In His earthly life our Lord gave Himself to the woman wasted with twelve years of sickness, to the sheep bleating piteously in the thicket, to the bruised reeds and the feebly smoking flax. So it is now when weakness appeals to Him; the weaker your faith the more likely you are to get a swift and sufficient answer.

I know very well how hopeless it seems ever to conquer where you have so often failed. Your own energy and natural force can never meet the case; but this is the province of the Saviour. The whole need not the physician, but they that are sick; and

He comes to make the sick whole. Believe that in Him is the complement of your need; that He does more than heal, because He can make what used to be your weakness your strength, and what had been your perpetual failure the most noticeable grace in your character. It seems impossible, but to God all things are possible.

> "The most impossible of all
>   Is that from sin I e'er should cease;
> Yet shall it be—I know it shall!
> Jesus, look to Thy faithfulness!
> Since nothing is too hard for Thee,
> All things are possible to me."

Then take up your bed and walk. Do not attempt to put forth this limb or the other to see if He has imparted strength enough. This is to distrust Him. Believe that He has healed you. Act faith. Start upon the level on which you would live if you *felt* entirely whole. He has made you whole if you have truly trusted Him, though you do not as yet feel it. Take up your bed, the emblem of your helpless paralysis; wrap it together—you need it no more. It has carried you; now carry it. You need go to no man to put you into the pool; you have Christ. You require no longer the angel-stirred pool; you are possessed of a life which is independent of the stirrings of God's angels. You *are* whole;

"WILT THOU BE MADE WHOLE?" 25

live a whole life in the power of the spirit of life which is in Christ Jesus.

This more than anything else will convince men and prepare them to listen to your testimony for your Saviour: that you should stand where you have so often fallen; that you should overcome where you have so often been defeated. But this new life shall be yours through the grace of Jesus communicated to your faith, as you abide in Him and He abides in you.

IV

"WHEN I HAD CEASED FROM MY STRUGGLES"

"Therefore will the Lord wait, that He may be gracious unto you."—ISA. XXX. 18.

THERE is nothing else for you but to come to this. As long as you wrestle with God you miss His richest blessings. Your hands are so occupied with your grasping and wrenching that they are not open enough to receive His choice bestowments of life and peace. Jacob wrestled with God the whole night and was no further advanced. It was when he could wrestle no more, because the sinew of his strength was shriveled, and he was near falling, and clung to the angel helpless and exhausted, that he received the blessing which made him a prince for the remainder of his days.

Is not this the mistake of your life? You have fought for the blessing; with strong cryings and tears you have made supplication and sought to prevail; you have been almost angry because you could not get what others had. Now lie down at the feet of Christ, a broken and emptied vessel, and see if He will not take you in hand and fill you to overflowing. "By strength shall no man prevail." "Not of works, lest any man should boast."

Suppose a man inexperienced to the water were drowning, how would you save him? Would you dare to put yourself in the way of his hands? Were you to do so he would drag you with him to the bottom. As long as he struggles you can do little for him; you must swim around in easy reach till he is exhausted and about to sink in despair, then you come up from behind and support him through the water to the land. That is how God acts. He *waits* that He may be gracious (Isa. xxx. 18). You think that He takes no notice of your tears and prayers and agonies. Ah, but He does! And He is not waiting because wanting in grace. He is waiting that He may show it. He cannot show His grace till you lie low and broken and helpless at His feet; then He will say, "I am thy salvation."

This is wonderfully illustrated in that chapter of Isaiah. Shebna and other Hebrew politicians were extremely anxious to form a great confederation of contiguous states to oppose the growing power of Assyria, which had already carried Samaria into captivity and was threatening the remoter kingdoms as with the long arms of an octopus.

At the time of which Isaiah writes ambassadors were crossing the strip of desert between Canaan and Egypt—the home of the young lion and flying serpent—to negotiate an alliance with the reigning dynasty of the Pharaohs. A graphic picture is given of the asses and camels laden with treasure patiently plodding their way over the heavy sands. Against this confederacy Isaiah protested with all his might. In his judgment it was a denial of Jehovah's protectorate; it was an unworthy appeal to worldly alliances; it was a policy foredoomed to fail. "For Egypt helpeth in vain, and to no purpose: therefore have I called her Rahab that sitteth still" (R. V.). "Woe to the rebellious children, saith the Lord, that take counsel, but not of Me; and that make a league, but not of My spirit."

But Isaiah was not satisfied with denouncing the wrong; he vehemently entreated them to return to rest, and repent and believe, to give up Egypt and trust simply in the living God. He said that God was not unmindful of their needs, and was only waiting till they had abandoned all their own efforts and endeavors, and were willing to let Him save them in His own way. "Therefore will the Lord wait, that He may be gracious unto you: . . . blessed are all they that wait for Him."

How truly is this applicable to you!

To those who are burdened with a sense of sin. You have been trying, like Christian, to rid yourself of your burden, and have been to Mr. Worldly Wiseman, to Madame Bubble, and to Mount Sinai. You have piled up penance and almsgiving and good works. You have agonized and wrestled and entreated, but all has been in vain. Now to quiet. Your gigantic struggles have been drawing the knots tighter. Be still and know that God can save you. He has been waiting all this while to save you, and as soon as you come to an end of yourself He will begin. He is exalted that He may have mercy—exalted to the cross and to the throne. He will be very gracious at the voice of thy cry.

It is told of Sancho Panza, in the great Spanish story, that he hung for hours to a window-ledge, fearing to lose his hold lest he should drop through many yards and be maimed for life, and when, after much anguish, he could hold out no longer, and dropped, it was only a few inches and he had reached the ground. So you have only to let yourself go, and you will find the everlasting arms just beneath.

To those who are seeking rest. We often seek rest in the wrong way. We think we must go down lower into humiliation, or climb up into a higher experience. We go backward and forward like birds that have got imprisoned in a room, and persist in flying to and fro, refusing to let themselves be caught by the hand which longs to capture them only to fling them out through the window into the sunny air.

It is just ceasing from your own works. The whole secret is in that word "cease." He that hath entered into God's rest *ceases* from his own works as God did from His. Cease from self, from your own endeavors after rest, from going after this teacher and the other; sink down like a tired child on the pillow of God's loving care. Lean back on God. God loves; God cares; God will interpose when the right moment is come. God will do the very best that can be done. He is waiting to do it as soon as you will let Him. Trust and rest.

To those who are seeking deliverance from besetting sin, or a holier life, or success in Christian work. There is but one law for all experiences. It is not of him that willeth or of him that runneth, but of God that showeth mercy. God longs to deliver from besetting sin; longs to lead to a life of full consecration and Holy Spirit possession; longs to make the utmost use of each vessel whom He has purchased. He waits to be gracious. But His loving work is in suspense until the excitement, the oscillation, the restless fever is subdued.

Call back the ambassadors from Egypt; break off the coalition with the Gentiles; call in your thoughts. Isaac Taylor said of his sister that she refused invitations to friends' houses when death was drawing near, in order that she might call home her thoughts. Call home your thoughts and be still. Rest in the Lord and wait patiently for Him. Be silent to Him. So He will be gracious. This is His method. He is a God of judgment, i.e., of method. Comply with His method, and His grace will flow to you as a river.

V

"BID ME COME!"

"Lord, if it be Thou, bid me come unto Thee on the water."—MATT. XIV. 28.

CHRIST comes to us all—to the gutter child prompted to divide her taffy with her little brother; to the girl following an ideal purity through the polluting associations of some miserable home; to the man of business who turns aside from the selfish maxims of his competitors to succor a comrade overtaken by misfortune; to the heathen catching sight of some loftier truth than the priests of idolatry ever taught him, and following it like a white bird. To all such, and, indeed, to all men, He comes, who as the true Light lighteth every man coming into the world.

To some He comes in the spring of life, when the number of the days behind is few and of those before many; He descends the woodland glade, the piles of deep soft moss muffling His footfall, the flowers springing back from His light tread. He makes His presence known in the caress of the mother pleading with her child to give its heart to the Master of life, in the word of the teacher or minister. To others He comes in summertide, as life is reaching its prime and thought is becoming mature, and when opportunity has been given to compare between a life full of accessories apart from Him, and one with Him apart from all accessories, and between these two the choice has been clearly and deliberately made.

Probably Christ oftenest comes through the night and storm, when the wind is contrary and the strength giving out, when the sky is black with the hurrying clouds, and the wind churns the water into a yeasty foam; when the hopes of former years have been disappointed, and the light that shone so brightly has faded; when ill health oppresses, when heart and flesh fail, when our days are bereft of the souls that made them speed quick as a meteor flash; when the fire burns low in the grate, when sin and sorrow have played sad havoc with us—then our troubles and losses make the pavement of His feet, and through the storm, nay, by means of the storm, the Master says, "I have come."

At first, it may be, Christ is only a vision, a new hope, a ship that may come within hail, a probability, an *if*. We have heard of the great things He has done for others; we have been arrested by the beauty of His portrait in the gospels; we have dreamed of Him as a radiant being, with the power of distributing healing and help. We would like to believe in Him and to learn those deep secrets which have lit up the lives of so many around. We feel that if we could but once get to His side He would answer our questions, realize our ideals, satisfy our passionate craving for love; and therefore, though we cling to the boat, and to the comrades whose toils we have been sharing, we finally resolve to make the venture. When a lull comes in the howl of the wind we say faintly, "If it be Thou, bid me come."

There is this beauty about the dealings of Christ our Saviour: He does not tantalize us, presenting an ideal or a vision of a better life which He will not or cannot communicate. The very idea of His incarnation was that He should set us an example that we should follow in His steps. If He lived wholly for God, we can; if He spent much time in prayer, we may; if He bore the contradiction of sinners against Himself without a single word of recrimination, it is possible for us to do so; if out of death He became fruitful of life, there is no reason why our death should not have a similar issue; if He walks the water, we may be sure it is not His intention merely to dazzle or startle us, as the acrobats at some country fair the open-eyed villagers, but that we may come to Him and walk with Him on the waves. It is always right to say to Jesus, "Where Thou art I would be; what Thou art doing I would do; where Thy feet are mine would find a foothold. Bid me come!"

Bid me come in the life of filial trust. Christ's life was as free from care as that of the bees among the limes. Amid the strife of men and the fret of daily circumstance He leaned back on the bosom of God; never alone, because the Father was with Him; never in need which the Father would not supply; always at rest, ever serene and tranquil, perpetually hidden in the secret of the divine tabernacle from the strife and babble of human tongues. Ah, exquisite vision! We see the life gliding over the waves that threaten to engulf us. We wish that it might be ours. But let us not be content with longings and regretful contrasts; let us say, "Bid me come, that my life may drink deep into Thy spirit, and keep step with Thee over the water."

Bid me come in the life of prayer. In this our Lord might have done less than we, but probably He did more. Amid His activities He always made time for the mountain height; amid His sufferings it was in prayer that He found solace and strength; amid the many demands that laid their withered hands upon His garment's hem, it was in prayer that He replenished the virtue that was always streaming out. From His own exercises He gathered the exhortations and precepts which have opened the way of prayer for His followers. Here again the radiant vision comes across the sea of time—so calm amid the storm, so elevated above the waves. And we do well to ask Him to empower us to pray as He did. Bid us come! Teach us to pray! Help us to leave the formal, careless prayers of the past, and to step out into fellowship with Thy mighty intercessions.

Bid me come to the same pitch of holy devotion and consecration. There was no pause in His life of devotion to His Father's will— always the devoted Servant, ever the obedient Son, instant in season and out of season to do the work with which the Father had intrusted Him. With steadfast face He made for His cross; with unswerving purpose He accomplished our redemption. We might well wish for this. Days in which the high purpose of our life has faltered come back to memory; hours when we have sunk down wearily to indolence and lethargy; moments when we have looked back to the cities of the plain, unable to face the rugged path of the cross. What a contrast between that heroic figure pressing through the storm, and the vacillation which has made us shrink from entering into conflict with its fury! "Bid us come" is a prayer which we do well to offer. His commands are enablings. With His word there goes power. Whatever He says to us we can do. Bid us come!

In all time of our tribulation bid us come to Thee for patience. In all time of our wealth bid us come to Thee for humility. In the hour of temptation bid us come to Thee for succor. In the hour when faith is small bid us come to Thee for strength. And in the solemn moment when we stand on the confines of time bid us come to Thee across the space of dark water, that where Thou art we may be also.

In all such coming there must be leaving. We must come down out of the boat. With some that boat represents prejudice; with others mistrust. The self-life in one of its many forms is as dear to us as that boat to Peter. Our resolutions and energies and endeavors appear at times to be the only plank between us and destruction. But as long as we hold on to any one of these we inevitably miss the freedom, luxury, and glory of walking with Christ on the waves. Who would not prefer the freedom of the sea-bird's flight to the narrow confinement of the creaking boat? Yet such is the contrast between faith and sight, between a life of fellowship with the risen Saviour and one of toiling in rowing. What is better, then, than to lift perpetually the cry, as any vision of Christ passes across our mind, "If it be Thou, bid me come unto Thee on the water"?

VI

NOT "ATTAIN," BUT "OBTAIN"

"I am come that they might have life."—JOHN X. 10.

A YOUNG Christian girl told me recently that she entered the life of unbroken fellowship and victory by noticing the distinction between these two words. For years she had been endeavoring to attain to a certain standard of rest and peace and power, but each year she seemed to get farther from the mark. One evening, however, she happened, as we say, to go to a little prayer-meeting, at which there were only three persons present besides the minister who was conducting it. While giving out a hymn he quietly looked up and said, "You see, my friends, this is something which we cannot attain, but must obtain." From that moment she saw that all that was needful for the noblest life had been accomplished and won by the Saviour, and that she had only to receive. From that moment an exceeding great light has filled her soul.

Perhaps the distinction will help some of my readers. You will never get the blessedness for which you long by struggling and agonizing, by your vehement cries and prayers, by your determined resolutions and endeavors; but by stilling yourself before God, and quietly appropriating the abundance of grace and of the gift of righteousness, which are in Christ Jesus.

Did you attain forgiveness and salvation at the outset of your Christian life by an effort of yours? Certainly you did not. You may have tried to do so for long years, but no peace or joy came; you became more miserable and hopeless; the wicket-gate and its shining light were farther off than ever. At last, when you had come to an end of yourself, one day you looked up and saw Jesus standing, and He offered you, without money and without price, without any equivalent on your part, forgiveness, righteousness, peace, and joy. You simply received. You took what He offered; you obtained as a gift what you could never have attained as a guerdon. This is precisely the attitude you must adopt with respect to all other gifts and graces in Christian living.

You cannot *attain* that victory over besetting sin which shall enable you to walk worthy of the gospel and of your Lord; you have fought and wrestled for it in vain for

NOT "ATTAIN," BUT "OBTAIN" 41

years and always been worsted. But you can *obtain* it by the up-glance of the eye of faith to the Lord Jesus, who has overcome all our foes, and holds in His hand the talisman of victory.

You cannot *attain* that power in service before which hard hearts will break and eyes unused to weeping shall be filled with tears. It is not an acquisition or an attainment; it will not come by practice, or education, or any number of elocution lessons; it is a secret from all who desire it for any selfish or vainglorious end. But if you will wait before God in silence and patience, your eyes being ever toward the Lord, He will give you your heart's desire.

You cannot *attain* some grace of Christian character which you long to possess, but you can *obtain* it. It is there, in the character of Jesus, waiting for you, and all that is requisite on your part is to adopt an attitude of utter and constant dependence. God has blessed us with *all* spiritual blessings in Jesus, and He hath given us all things that pertain to life and godliness through the blessed knowledge of the Son of His love.

How could I answer such a letter as the following unless I knew this blessed secret? "Five years ago," the writer says, "I got into a very bad habit, which I did not take much notice of then, but which has clung to me ever since. I find that it has a very much stronger hold than formerly, and all my efforts to throw it off seem to be useless. I have made special prayers to God for the past two years, asking Him to give me strength to overcome the temptation. I get very disheartened, for it seems that my prayers are not heard, and I seem to be getting worse rather than better. Now will you please tell me what I can do?"

Now there is only one thing to say: "Do not strive to attain the victory by your own efforts, but look to Jesus to *give* the victory." "Now thanks be to God, who *giveth* us the victory through our Lord Jesus Christ." "They that *receive* the abundance of grace shall reign."

To live like this is very blessed. The heart is stilled in its great expectancy. It realizes that all it needs is in God, and it endeavors to live with nothing between itself and the Source of all its bliss and grace. Then as each emergency, trial, or difficulty arises it simply goes to the everlasting supply which God has caused to reside in Jesus, and obtains all, and more than all, its desire.

VII

AT THE GATE OF THE WILL

" Oh, keep my soul, and deliver me!"—Ps. xxv. 20.

THERE was a castle once, the key to a system of national defense. It was often beleaguered by its foes, who invested it on all sides, allowing no chance of attack to pass without pressing for an advantage over the defenders. It had not, however, so much to fear around its walls, since it was strongly fortified—nature and art having combined to render it a stronghold; but its weakness lay in the great entrance-gate, through which was ingress and egress between the castle and the surrounding country. Through this gate the enemy had often poured, carrying it by storm, to be driven out with great difficulty after wreaking their vindictive malice on the fabric. When times were troublous and an attack was expected, elaborate care was taken to strengthen this gateway and, above all, to strictly scrutinize all who passed in and out. But often it happened that the traitors flocked into the old keep amid the crowds that passed to and fro, hiding themselves in the precincts until a signal was given from without, when they betrayed the castle to its foes. Stricter and ever stricter watch was instituted by the garrison, but the traitors were so wily that, like the Gibeonites of old, they disguised themselves. They assumed the garb of loyal subjects, and seemed engaged in innocent and natural pursuits, and so eluded scrutiny. It was only after repeated failure that finally the garrison intrusted the keeping of that gate to one of the most experienced officers of the royal court, who was well accustomed to detect the presence of the enemy under every disguise. He from that day forward kept the closest watch, and often arrested an apparently harmless individual who, on being searched, turned out to be a spy or an incendiary. Under his watchful care the castle was kept from fear of surprise and he was able also to repel many an assault.

This is a thinly veiled parable of the heart, young reader. It is a stronghold which God has intrusted to our care; but Satan beleaguers it and is ever seeking to win it for himself. The one point, however, which is most vulnerable is the great gate of the will. If only that were always kept closely shut against the foe, whether in disguised or open attack, we might safely defy all the power of

AT THE GATE OF THE WILL 45

the enemy, so strict is the partition between our human nature and diabolic hate. But it is just there that we are weakest. The keeper of that gate has often been bribed by the imagination, after it has been over-persuaded and induced, in spite of the remonstrances of the judgment, to admit certain thoughts which sought for admission, but which have perpetrated nameless outrages. We have weakly yielded in the suggestion. The gates have been thrown open, to our awful hurt.

If we could only stop bad thoughts from entering the precincts of the soul, how safe and happy we should be! We could easily enough ward off assaults from without if we were not betrayed from within. But we should not be betrayed there if only we were more careful and resolute in examining, searching, and turning back the subtle and evil suggestions which knock for admittance.

Think of the zealous care with which the Czar of all the Russias is surrounded. No stranger could enter his palace. The highest-born have to pass through a strict cordon of scrutiny ere they are admitted to the imperial presence. And this is necessary if he is to be preserved from the plots of the nihilists, from dynamite or cold steel. If his palace were left as unwatched as we leave our hearts,—if it were as easy for traitors to enter as it is for thoughts or evil imaginations to intrude within our souls,—his life would be instantly forfeited. But if we exercised the same unsleeping vigilance over every thought, suggestion, fancy, or ambition, the soul might be left as pure and safe as the Kremlin during the late celebrations.

Do you not know this? All temptation begins with the first flitting thought, which shows itself like the air of a fugue—merely a suggestion, a fancy, a desire. It seems innocent enough. You are disposed to admit it. Why shouldn't you? It is surely needless to make too much ado about what seems so innocent, or at least so trifling. And that thought may lie in your heart, like a spore of contagion in the system, for days or even months without revealing its malign intention. Then, some day when you least expect it, it will suddenly leap out, full-armed, upon you, like the warriors from the wooden horse which the Trojans, in an evil hour, drew within their gates. Every temptation begins in the first faint suggestion. Deal with that and no power of the adversary can prevail against you. Yield to that and sooner or later you will rue your weakness and find that the innocent-looking egg contained a viper, and that the tiny, trickling streamlet has become a raging torrent which carries all before it in its ungovernable passion.

If only each young soul that reads this page would realize this! Keep your thoughts and you keep your hearts. Indulge suspicious or evil thoughts and you cannot hope to prevail in the conflict against sin.

But of course the difficulty arises at the gate of the soul. We are so weak. Frequent yielding in the past has robbed us of much of the power of resistance. We are so easily deceived; we do not detect the traitor; we admit the crowd of visitants so easily. The stream is always pouring in and out, and we cannot or will not use all our powers in discriminating and winnowing the bad from the good.

For this reason there is nothing for it but to intrust the keeping of our souls to our Saviour, who will gladly undertake the charge. Ask Him to place a strong warder at the gate of the will,—one beyond suspicion and incapable of being bribed,—who shall detect in a moment and beneath every disguise the unhallowed and treacherous impulse, and shall have strength enough to repel. There is no doubt who that warder will be. The Holy Spirit alone is equal to so difficult and important a work. But when the soul is intrusted to Him there is no fear of failure. Live in the Spirit, walk in the Spirit, and you shall not fulfil the lusts of the flesh.

Would that I had words to burn this

thought into every heart! Thoughts are always trooping up to the gate of the soul— happy and sad, of home and love and business, which recall the past and anticipate the future, some dressed in fustian, others in gold and silver tissue. Now in that crowd, under a harmless exterior, evil and traitorous thoughts often mingle and pass in without much notice or resistance on our part. If only we would yield ourselves to the Holy Spirit! He would not prohibit anything that was natural and innocent, but would detect, expose, and put back all that was not pure, holy, lovely, and of good report. Then peace and blessedness and salvation would reign through the whole fortress of man-soul.

VIII

THE CONTROL OF OUR THOUGHTS

"Bringing into captivity every thought to the obedience of Christ."—2 COR. x. 5.

UNTIL you have learned to control your thoughts you will never be able to live a godly and righteous life. As a man thinketh in his heart so is he, and it is because the thoughts that we entertain in the hostelry of the soul are such worthless and vain ones that our words and acts often bring so heavy a disgrace on the Name we love. Well might the wise man say, "Keep thy heart with all diligence; for out of it are the issues of life" (Prov. iv. 23). When the heart is right the ear (20) and the eye (21) and the mouth (24) and the foot (27) will necessarily obey its promptings; but when the heart is wrong, filled with tides of ink, like the cuttlefish, it will envelop itself in the impurity to which it gives vent.

There are many who pride themselves on

their outward behavior—on not having invaded the rights of God or man; they even bear a Christian name and are engaged in Christian work, but their minds are full of lewd and vile thoughts which desecrate the sacred precincts of the soul, that was meant to be alone the temple of God. Thus the beasts driven into the temple courts filled them with their stench and demanded the interposition of Christ. Does your heart conform to the Master's description of the house in which there is no part dark, or is it like some gloomy cave in which slimy things crawl at their will? If the latter,—if you habitually permit evil things to have right of way through you or lodging within you,—remember that in God's sight you are held equally guilty as those who indulge in evil acts, because you are withheld, not by your fear of Him, but by your desire to maintain your position among men. That you know the better and yet secretly allow the worse only aggravates your sin in His sight, to which all things are naked and open. Remember also that the secret working of evil thoughts will inevitably show itself sooner or later, just as the insidious work of the white ant in the wood will prepare for the sudden collapse of the house.

Do not say that you cannot control your thoughts. It is perfectly certain that you can. It would be true for you to say that you had not controlled them. Your mind has sadly resembled a public house, whose swing-doors on the level of the pavement make it so easy of access for every passer-by. You have allowed any thought that chose to enter and tell its tale, like the pilgrims in Chaucer's masterpiece. Now it is perfectly certain that we all have the God-given power of excluding bad and vain thoughts, or of turning toward whatsoever things are true, honorable, just, pure, lovely, gracious. "If there be any virtue, and if there be any praise, *think on these things*."

Suppose there is some one evil thought which is always haunting you, coming back perpetually, spreading itself between you and everything as a blue mist, poisoning the springs of love, life, and simple, natural enjoyment. You should label it, stamp it with the brand of your moral censure and disapprobation. Say, "This is an evil, hell-born thought." Place it beneath the ban of your steadfast excommunication. What will be the result? Every time it occurs you will remember what you have thought and said of it. Like Cain, it will bear the mark of the curse wherever it comes. As soon as it shadows your path or puts its head in through the swinging doors, you will accost it as a criminal and bid it begone. There are men who have done this with their dreams. Before sleeping they have said to themselves, "If such or such visions dare to force their way through the curtains of the night, they are burglars come to steal peace, purity, and heaven." Such a thought has aroused them from their slumbers; with a start they have awoke to detect the stealthy tread of the intruder, and to bid him begone in the name of God.

All this gains additional emphasis in the light of Christ. He counts evil thoughts as traitors not only to us, but to Himself. Like the psalmist, we may say, "I hate vain thoughts," not only because of the curse they bring to my heart, but for the grief they give to my King. Their intrusion is forbidden by the double barrier of our own choice and, more than all, of the keeping power of Jesus. Let the peace of God keep the door of heart and mind, scrutinizing each intruder and turning back the unfit. Let the Holy Spirit bring every thought into captivity to the obedience of Christ. Let the faithful Saviour have the keeping of the soul intrusted to Him, that He may watch every menacing thought which lurks in the shadow or steals up the glen. He is well able to keep what is committed to Him. He will not fail the suppliant whose lips are familiar with one of the greatest of uninspired prayers: "Cleanse the thoughts of our hearts by the inspiration of Thy Holy Spirit, that we may perfectly love Thee and worthily magnify Thy holy name." If only you would ask Christ to undertake the straining out of unworthy, vain, proud, jealous, and evil thoughts, you would find that He would be as vigilant as the warder who from his watch-tower detects the spy or traitor.

Then, as to the control of good thoughts, each of us has the power of arresting a current of thinking and of turning the attention to some new subject or topic of interest. It has been recommended that we should carry about a little card with four or five words written clearly upon it, each being associated with some tender or startling memory,—such as mother, the name of some pure, sweet child, the place of a great deliverance, the date of some miraculous interposition,—so that a new train of thought might be suggested and the mind be filled with light and love. Some of those who have adopted this plan have spoken warmly of its advantages. They have related how, in moments when the rabble rout of evil imaginations was bursting into the soul, deliverance was wrought through the angel form of some holy memory.

Let this be as it may, there is surely a more excellent way. If any name is an amulet against evil or an incentive to holy thinking, the name of JESUS will best meet the requirements of the soul's urgency. There is no name like His. Blessed Spirit, remind us of it, and when passion begins to rise and howl without like the winter's wind, stand within our heart and speak the Name which is above every name, till the storm subsides and there is a great calm.

There is something better still. Let us abide in Christ, so that He shall become the very element of our existence, permeating and penetrating our inner nature. Where His life is strong within us it will be as sensitive of the least approach of evil as the mirror in the ancient fable detected the slightest taint of imposture and falsehood. When His life is strong within us it will repel everything that is alien to itself with a repugnance and swiftness that shall admit of no remonstrance. When His life is strong within us it will control all imaginings and thinkings, subjecting them to His sway, transfiguring them with His light, yoking them to the chariot of His victorious progress.

IX

NOT JOY, BUT CHRIST

"Follow on to know the Lord."—Hos. vi. 3.

I AM constantly meeting people who complain that the joy experienced by them in their consecration to God has faded away after the first few days, like light fades off a landscape; and they complain bitterly, as if they had receded from the position which they had taken up, and in seeking their lost joy they become involved in deeper darkness. We may become as much self-centered in our search for joy as we are in our search for salvation.

Of course there may be reasons for this loss of rapture, and these should be dealt with. One of these may be the trust in the impetus received at the moment, instead of the constant clinging to Christ—as if a number of railway carriages could suppose that a rapid run of several miles would suffice to carry them for coming hours in complete independence of the engine. Or, again, we may suppose that we can do with less fellowship with Christ through His Word, whereas, in point of fact, the consecrated soul needs more; and, indeed, that consecration is spurious which does not lead to more. Or, again, there may be some laxity in applying to new events the principles assumed at the solemn moment of self-dedication.

But, supposing none of these causes apply, there is no reason for anxiety at the loss of emotion. Feeling comes and goes, but the facts of spiritual experience are permanent. The nature of man cannot be always yielding crops of ecstatic pleasure. Like the fields of nature, the heart of man must lie fallow. Tides must ebb after their flow. But all this does not affect by a single iota the position of the will to be only for Jesus. And it is a blessed thing to look up into His face and say, "I do not feel as I did, but I am precisely as I was when I felt most."

This search for highly kindled feeling is a mistake, and it is the source of perplexity and trouble to numberless souls. We have to seek, not feeling, but to know Christ, to do Christ's will, to keep His commandments, to be conformed to His image. If feeling comes as the result of any of these things, welcome it as God's most precious kiss of approval; but if it do not come, dare to believe that God is equally pleased, even though He withhold the sense of His warm embrace.

Let us "follow on to know the Lord." Let us count all things but loss for the excellency of His knowledge. Let us make every endeavor to grow in grace and in the knowledge of our God and Saviour. In doing this we must be content to pass through times of comparative darkness. You cannot know the sadder aspects of Christ's character unless you are prepared to go with Him into the shadow. His path lies now, as formerly, through Gethsemane with its somber shadows, beneath the weight of the cross, and down into the grave. To know Him under these circumstances demands a curtaining of the soul from the full blaze of the sun of unbroken rapture. Christ is the Man of Sorrows, and the Lamb slain, and the High Priest touched with the feeling of our infirmities; and there must be a stepping down with Him into the shadowed valley if we are to know some of the innermost aspects of His nature. Paul spoke about "the fellowship of His sufferings" and "conformity to His death."

Flowers will not reach their perfection if they are kept always in a place of light, natural and artificial, and there are lessons to be learned and virtues to be acquired which are incompatible with a highly exalted state of emotional rapture. Light is *sown* for the righteous, and sowing time is the stripping time of the dank autumn days, with the fallen leaves bestrewing the forest glade. There are plenty that like the glad harvest of light, but are unwilling to pay the price.

His coming forth is prepared, not only as the morning, but as the rain; and the rain means clouds, and the clouds mean brooding shadows. But Jesus is in the rain and the shadow as much as in the light that breaks from the east at dawn. Ah, soul! thou wouldest always have Him come with the radiant glow of His transfiguration fresh upon Him; but a greater miracle was wrought when He crossed the sea in the storm, and they knew not that it was He, because the mists had veiled His figure.

It is consistent with Scripture and experience to believe that the soul may be at perfect rest and peace, unruffled and permanent through every phase of feeling. This is blessedness. This is the heritage of every true servant of Christ, like the rock which remains steadfast amid the ebb and flow of the tide. Young believers, cling to this as your inalienable portion.

But while this peace is possible, a highly wrought emotional rapture is neither healthy nor needful. Still, whether it is present or not, the one thing is to abide in the will of

God and to find our peace in fulfilling the somber bits of the plan as well as the brighter, gayer ones, leaving it for Him to put gladness into our hearts if we can learn more of Him so, or sadness if thus we can make more rapid progress toward His ideal.

"For he, and he only, with wisdom is blest,
   Who, gathering true pleasures wherever they grow,
Looks up in all places for joy or for rest,
   To the Fountain whence Time and Eternity flow."

X

THE HOUR OF TEMPTATION

"God will not suffer you to be tempted above that ye are able."—1 COR. X. 13.

TEMPTATION is the trying or testing of the soul. Satan tempts with evil to make us fall; God tries us by putting into our lives occasions for laying aside evil and engaging in heroic acts for Him. We have thus the frequent opportunity of learning what is really in our hearts and of stepping up into a sweeter, purer, stronger life.

Every pure soul is an offense to every evil one, and therefore those who are themselves evil are always endeavoring to drag down the good to their own infamous level. Perhaps there is a deeper reason why the Christian soldier is beset by the principalities and powers of darkness. The devil and all his demon emissaries hate Jesus Christ with a malignity and fury that flame the more intensely as they know their efforts against Him are futile. They cannot reach Him; the

THE HOUR OF TEMPTATION

Father has put them under His feet in the mighty victory of the cross and the ascension; He sits at the right hand of power, all rule and principality and power being beneath Him forever; so they seek to strike at Him by striking at those who believe in Him. Therefore the glory of Jesus Christ is involved in every temptation by which we are threatened, and for His sake, if not for our own, we must stand firm.

Do not think that temptations prove that you are deteriorating in the divine life. On the contrary, the fierce temptation of the wilderness succeeds immediately on the opened heaven and the voice of God. Have you been declared to be the beloved son of God? Then the Spirit will drive you into the wilderness to be tempted of the devil, as though by suffering the blessed revelation shall be wrought more deeply into the fabric of the soul. The more ripe fruit there is in the orchard of your heart the more violent will be the attempt to steal it. The closer you are identified with your Captain in the thickest of the fight the more will be your exposure to the heaviest fire of the foe.

God permits us to be tempted. The Evil One is always considering the saints, as he did Job; but he cannot approach them unless God permit, and that permission is not given unless our Father knows that we have grace enough to withstand. The pressure of temptation is always carefully adjusted to our power of resistance. He is faithful and will not suffer us to be tempted beyond what we are able to bear, but with the temptation will send us His all-sufficient grace or show the way of escape (2 Cor. xii. 9). Our Lord taught us to ask that we should not be led into temptation; therefore we know that if we are led in we shall be sustained in the fight and led out without a scratch.

God is our Father and loves us infinitely; there must therefore be the best of reasons why we are so frequently exposed to the fierce ordeal of temptation. Is it to burn in the colors His Spirit lays on us, as men do with porcelain? Is it to teach us the art of spiritual warfare, to make our sinews lissome, our eye quick, our frame agile, as lads are trained in the gymnasium or fencing-school? Is it to force us by our very necessities to avail ourselves of His succoring might? This at least is clear: there is no necessity for us to fall or sin before temptation. Our Lord was tempted in all points like as we are, yet without sin. It were possible for a soul to go through hell itself so full of the love of God, so environed by His protection, that it would come out on the other side without even a hair singed or the smell of fire upon it.

The devil likes to find us alone. Seclusion

in the caves of the Thebaid did not relieve the old hermits from the assaults of evil, but rather intensified them. When Eve was apart from Adam the serpent spoke to her; Jesus was alone when the devil came to Him. Beware, then, of hours of solitude, but know that your Father is in secret. Cry to Him and He will be your very present help.

The power of the tempter lies in surprise. No bell rings in heaven to tell us that the dark squadrons are stealing around our castle. No storm-signal hangs out to warn against the approaching depression. Only the watcher angel that loves us, and certainly the good Shepherd who pleads for us now as for Peter on Olivet, detect the stealthy approach of the enemy of our souls. Let us watch, therefore, and pray, lest we enter into temptation. I have invariably found that when I have congratulated myself on being secure from any special form of temptation I have been exposed to its full fury within twenty-four hours.

If you carefully watch yourselves you will find that *failure in temptation is always preceded by some permitted evil* which took place perhaps days before. The final assault is sudden, but the sappers and miners had been at work long before. The tree fell unexpectedly in the hurricane which swept over the forest in the night, but the borer-worm had been at its heart for weeks before the final crash. Peter's fall was prepared by the dispute in the upper chamber as to the greatest. Be very careful against the slight spores of disease that float in the air and insinuate themselves into the system; so only will you escape in the epidemic. The first flitting suggestion, the thought which is inserted into the heart,—as thieves put a trained child in at a window that it may go round to open the door to the gang,—the permitted look of desire—these are to be feared, because they breed in the nest of the heart. Listen to the genealogy of evil: "Lust, when it hath conceived, beareth sin: and sin, when it is full-grown, bringeth forth death" (James i. 15).

Yielding is the result of previous decline. The sin that breaks into manifestation, bad and black as it is, and needing confession and restoration, has far-reaching roots; and to be dealt with properly we must not only confess the one act, but go back to the first evil suggestion which we permitted to lie within us uncondemned. Bankruptcy is the climax of months of bad trading. Rapid consumption brings to light the disease which had long been undermining the system. Keep in perfect soul-health, robust and hearty, well nourished by the food of the Word, and inspiring deed breaths of the heavenly air, and you need fear no sudden shock of disease.

The tempted may dwell between double doors. First, he is in Christ; second, Christ is in him. If you are in Christ you are above the devil, for the devil is put under His feet. If, then, you are only at His feet you are above your great adversary. Abide in Christ. As long as you do you cannot sin consciously and wilfully. The whole energy of hell is to seduce men from abiding in Christ. If by permitted sin, by neglected Bible-reading, by rushing out after the sweetness of earth, by worrying as to the future, we leave our shelter in the clefts of the rock, we become an easy prey to Satan. But as long as we live in fellowship with Him, casting on Him our care, studying and feeding on His Word, living up to all known duty, and cultivating the spirit of charity to all, we remain inside our citadel and are safe.

Also, *Christ is in us* as a treasury of unknown grace and blessing, our light and salvation, our life and strength. If we cannot hold the door against the devil, the Stronger than he can do it for us, and will do at the feeblest call of our faith. Let us put Christ between us and temptation. Let us not be content with resistance, but take more of Christ's grace as the antidote; Christ's purity amid suggestions of impurity; Christ's strength in hours of fearfulness and trembling; Christ's meekness when tempted to pride or vainglory; Christ's gentleness when about to judge or act harshly; Christ's prayerfulness when thoughts wander and the soul cleaves with folded wing to the earth.

So shall be realized the ancient predictions of Psalm xci. Dwelling in the secret place of the Most High, and abiding under the shadow of the Almighty, there will be no reason why we should fear the terror by night or the arrow by day, the lion or adder, the young lion or the serpent. Only set your love on God and you shall be delivered.

XI

THE CONQUEROR FROM EDOM

"Mighty to save."—ISA. LXIII. 1-3.

ISRAEL and Edom were hereditary foes. This was the more remarkable because their ancestors were brothers. But from the earliest there was strife between these two, and the antagonism of the cradle was perpetuated throughout the history of the great nations which owed their existence to Jacob and Esau respectively.

When Israel pleaded for permission to pass through the land of Edom and so curtail the weary desert march, Edom refused and came out against him with much people and with a strong hand—an affront which was never forgotten. It was a grim satisfaction, therefore, to Israel when the whole band of Edom was temporarily subdued under David. But the subjection could not be maintained, and through the troubled reigns of the kings we find the Edomites always giving trouble, siding with Israel's inveterate foes, and taking every opportunity of molestation and injury. When Nebuchadnezzar made the final assault against the Holy City, it was the children of Edom who cried, "Raze it, raze it, even to the foundation thereof."

Esau may fairly be taken as an emblem of the imperious desires of the flesh that will hardly brook restraint, but lust against the spirit, fretting for their wild and unrestrained indulgence. For one morsel of meat he sold his birthright; and we all know moments when, for one brief spell of gratification, we are disposed to barter away our noblest prerogatives and squander our most sacred trust. Who has not stood between the basin of steaming pottage—which appeals so daintily to the hungry sense—and the power to pray, to know God, to bless mankind, which are the sacred prerogatives of the soul? Many a time has our choice wavered in the balance; and what was true years ago may perhaps be true still. Edom still vexes us and makes incursions into the sacred territory of the soul; the flesh is still vehement within us; the old Adam is more than a match for the young Melanchthon.

One day a novel and blessed spectacle greeted the prophet's gaze. Standing on the last ranges of the low hills which sloped down from Jerusalem toward the Edomite territories, he descried in the distance the figure of a mighty conqueror coming from Edom, with dyed garments from Bozrah, its capital city, glorious in his apparel, and traveling in the greatness of his strength. When within speaking distance he asked who it was, and received in answer the reply:

"The mighty Saviour!"

Again he asked the reason for the stains on his dress, as of the treader of grapes in the wine-press, receiving the reply:

"It is the life-blood of Israel's foes, the juice of the vintage of Edom."

From that moment Israel had no further need for alarm—from that quarter at least. There in the desert haze she could always descry the figure of that almighty Victor by whom Edom had been subdued. Her cities were in ruins, her palaces leveled to the ground, her soldiers had bitten the dust, and there was therefore now the most absolute security.

The lesson for ourselves is obvious and hardly needs enforcement. Jesus died in the likeness of sinful flesh; in dying it was rent. The rending veil of the temple and the rending flesh on the cross teach the same lesson —that Jesus mastered the flesh by the spirit, overcame it as He uttered His dying cry of victory, and in His resurrection came up from the Edom of our foes radiant with victory, though stained with the blood-juice of the battle.

Whatever the flesh means for any one of us, with its passion and pride, its self-assertion, its imperious will, its restless yearning for gratification and license—all has been met, vanquished, and forever trodden under foot by Him who is mighty to save and who travels in the greatness of His strength to succor the weakest and most often defeated of His disciples.

We need not fear the flesh if we abide in Jesus, because He has so absolutely encountered and mastered it, and if we abide in Him we share His victory. It is indeed as much ours as it is His. It is ours because we are one with Him. It was His that it might be ours. Let us meditate on this great fact until it has become part of the texture of our inner consciousness. Let us call to mind the special form of pride, selfishness, or self-indulgence that most perpetually masters us as Edom did Israel, and let us realize as a matter of fact, if not of feeling or consciousness, that this has been specifically encountered and mastered by our blessed Lord. It was included in the victory of Calvary. It was one of the cities or townships in that territory of Edom over which He cast out His shoe, and therefore, by virtue of union with Him in His glorious resurrection, it has no right for a single other moment to assert supremacy over those who live in vital and conscious fellowship with Him. It is a great point gained in the inner conflict to know that our Edom has been vanquished; to know that no proud lust is too strong for Jesus; to know that His victory was acquired for us and is ours if only we dare avail ourselves of its prevalence.

Whenever, then, the Edom of the flesh asserts itself, fall back on the victory of the cross, where Christ refused to listen to its solicitations, but laid down His life and gave Himself to the rending nail, the piercing spear. Identify yourself with that victory; believe that the body of sin has been done away—that we should no more be in bondage to sin. Assert your freedom and reckon that the living Saviour comes from your Edom, leaving it a defeated and devastated kingdom, mighty to save you to the uttermost since you have fled to Him for shelter, succor, and salvation.

As long as the soul maintains its position in the risen and victorious Son of God it is invulnerable. The flesh may chafe for its old supremacy, but in vain. It cannot pass across the great gulf of Christ's grave and resurrection; it cannot reassert its pristine power. The only way, therefore, in which Satan can succeed in bringing us again beneath the power of the flesh is either by hiding from us what Christ has done or by leading us to look away from it to the strength of the foe, the weakness of our might, the perpetual failures of the past.

"The flesh is so strong," the tempter says. "Look at it in its pride; is it likely that you will ever be able to master it?"

"You are so weak," the tempter suggests. "It is not to be supposed that you can hold your ground against so mighty and persistent an adversary."

"You have failed so often in the past. In spite of your most strenuous efforts and most solemn vows, you have failed and failed again. Each failure has weakened you. Is it likely that you can stand where you have so often fallen?"

If the soul listens to these suggestions and looks away from Jesus, it is tempted out of that abiding fellowship with Him through which it is made a participator of His victory. But if, on the other hand, it refuses to have its gaze diverted from the risen Lord; if it persists in its repose on His victorious might; if it dares to appropriate the position which pertains to all who believe, as seated in the heavenly places, far above all principality, and power, and might, and dominion—then the demand of the flesh sinks harmlessly into foam and dies away upon the shore on which, a moment before, it had thundered forth its demands.

This is the victory that overcomes, even our faith—faith in what Jesus is, faith in what He has done, faith in the might of His hand, the faithfulness of His heart, the tenacity of His love. Oh, heed His voice, weary, troubled heart! He speaks in righteousness and is mighty to save. Cherish the unfailing conviction that Jesus stands forevermore between thee and thy foes.

XII

OUR IDEALS

"Conformed to the image of His Son."—ROM. VIII. 29.

How much an ideal may do! When I was a little boy every one was talking of the Crimean War, the Malakoff, the Redan, Sebastopol. Now there was at the end of our playground an unsightly bank of earth. This, however, became to us lads a frowning fortress with massive walls and threatening cannon, and we were the Light Brigade. With horses beneath us and lances in rest, we charged and carried the grim old fortress every day between dinner and school. Ah, I was captain then, with a few trusty officers, and the weight of the campaign upon me. You tell me it was only a mud-bank and a playground. Nay, verily; it was a battle-field for all the world to me. The prosaic commonplace was idealized by the roseate hue of that young fancy which shed its glow on all.

OUR IDEALS

The little children gather and dance around the barrel-organs in our London streets. I always walk slower to watch the motions of their feet and the smile on their faces. Again they are idealizing. That sloppy street is a richly carpeted saloon, and they—little guttersnipes—are real ladies, and their fluttering rags are ball-dresses, and that untuneful clatter is a band! They could hardly be happier if their ideal were the reality, so strongly does it affect the reality.

It is very important to have a noble ideal. Suppose two young hearts begin to love, or that they have entered wedded life; is it not of inestimable importance to read to them those imperishable words in which Robert Browning declares his love to his wife, and she hers, and to remind them how he yearly kissed the steps of the church at Marylebone where they were wed, because she stepped up them to the marriage altar? Then the man takes on the ideal of Browning in his behavior toward the woman, and the woman thinks how a wife so loved must act.

Or suppose a young minister is tempted to indolence or unspirituality; is it not peremptory to raise his ideal? Give him the ideal of a McCheyne, a Brainerd, a Gordon; then, as he returns to a narrow sphere and awkward personalities and starved circumstances, he will conduct himself among them

with the air of God's own nobility. It may
be only a little chapel, but to him it will become a minster; through the scrapings of a
few violins he will hear the pealing notes of
the organ; and as he goes in and out among
the handful of poor people who compose his
charge the spirit of Elijah will rest on Elisha,
and his ideal will transform them into a
beautiful flock.

For many years General Gordon was my
ideal. How I read and read again the story
of his life and the inner story given in his
letters! That utter trust in God to fulfil
through him His divine purpose; that indifference to praise or blame so long as He
was pleased; that singleness of purpose, that
strength of soul, that humility which would
not keep the presents of the emperor lest
they should foster a spirit of ostentation!
For years I walked the battle-field of life as
he, with his slim walking-stick, the battle-fields of China and Egypt.

Young people, your lives may seem to be
prosaic and dull enough, your opportunities
limited, your associates and companions uninteresting; but in the midst of all you may
realize your ideals, you may pass as noble a
life as in a palace among the sweetest, noblest
souls. Life does not consist in what we have
or know or do, in the people about us, or the
drapery by which the bare facts of existence

are veiled, but in what we are. You may
make believe until what you believe in is
actually realized. Dare to believe that that
wilderness is a paradise and that dry land
springs of water, and you will soon find it
literally so.

But there is no ideal like that presented in
the character of the man Christ Jesus, no
motto so wholesome and inspiring as to ask,
"What would Jesus have done?" no ambition so ennobling as to walk through the
world being as absolutely Christlike as possible, so that weary and fallen souls may look
up to us and think that Christ has come again
to the world, and bless God for us. In Jesus
there is the complete ideal of human life:
of the Child at Nazareth, of the Servant in
the workshop, of the Lover in His affection
for His church, of the Friend, the Sufferer,
the Patriot, the Saviour. Let your spirit soak
itself in the thought of Jesus and go forth to
reproduce Him, till that employment become the carpenter's shop; that charge of
souls Capernaum or Jerusalem; that necessity
for strong, brave words the temple façade;
that perpetual source of anguish the glade
of Gethsemane.

Never spare yourself. Do not slur over
your failure to realize your ideal, as though
it were a trifling and insignificant matter.
Confess it to yourself, to your companion in

it, and, above all, to God. Nothing will so soon spoil the ear of the singer as inattention to minor inaccuracies of execution and expression. When once you permit yourself to fall beneath your best you begin to drift rapidly to the worst. Run not as uncertainly. Fight not as one beating the air. Strive as though life itself depended on winning the guerdon of success. Plenty of voices will urge you to spare yourself. Like Peter, our friends dissuade us from the cross: "This shall not be unto thee." Oh for grace to be merciless to ourselves!

If you fall, fall with your face still toward your ideal. Never give it up! Like the brave Scot, fling the heart of the Bruce forward into the battle and follow. The cliff towers far away into the blue, and you have tried many paths to scale it in vain, but there is a path that other men have trodden and succeeded. Never rest till you have found it and stand victorious.

Be very merciful to others. Compare their worst with your worst, and not, as so many do, other people's worst with your best. You cannot be blind to their faults, but you can be infinitely tender and compassionate. This will keep your heart sweet and young, like a spring of fresh water amid an ocean of brine. The most trying temperament with which you may be yoked will only bring out your noblest traits by giving them abundant exercise.

Above all, seek the grace and power of the Holy Spirit. He alone can give you the ideal, and He alone can enable you to plant the sprig of paradise in the unkindly soil of your heart and life and nurture it into a noble plant. He worketh in us to will and to do of His good pleasure. Only work out what He works in. Whenever the Holy Spirit definitely, earnestly, and persistently urges you in a certain direction, be sure to yield prompt obedience. If your will falters ask Him to work in you to will; if your power fails trust Him to work in you to work of His good pleasure. Be pliant and obedient and you shall eat the fruit of the land.

XIII

HOW TO RECEIVE

ROM. V. 11, 17.

THERE are two remarkable verses in Romans v. which employ this word "receive," and which hold the key of the richest, deepest, and most blessed life. The one tells us that we should *receive* the at-one-ment, and the other that we should *receive* the abundance of God's grace and reign in this mortal life as we hope one day to reign in the eternal life of heaven. We must not only ask, but receive; we must pass from seeking to finding; we must never leave the door till it has been opened to us.

There is a difference between supplication or entreaty and this attitude of our spirit. In the former we implore God to give us what we suppose can only be gained by the urgency of our entreaty; in the latter we take what, before we asked, God had placed within our reach. The beautiful garments had been prepared—it was for us to don them; the armor was at hand—it was for us to gird it on; the water of life was gushing at our feet—it was for us to dip it up.

It might be feared that words like these would lead some to spend less time in the prayer-closet than formerly. This might appear in theory, but it is not so in practice. On the contrary, there is more interest in our daily converse with God when we find that we are able to do definite transacting with Him, bring from His presence blessed and evident gifts, and store spiritual force in those sacred moments. The space once occupied by the vague entreaty or the vagrant impulse is now filled with adoration, or with thanksgiving for blessing received, or with intercession for others, and our heart becomes an altar from which the clear flame is ever ascending, with as little as possible of the more selfish and personal element.

It is noticeable that this word is most often used of the Holy Spirit. Comparatively rarely are we told to ask for Him; much more often are we bidden to *receive* Him by a living faith. "He breathed on them, and said, Receive ye the Holy Ghost."

Let us notice some conditions of the faculty of receptiveness.

1. *We must be still before God.* The life around is in this age preëminently one of rush and effort. It is the age of the express-train

and electric telegraph. Years are crowded into months and weeks into days. This feverish haste threatens the religious life. The stream has already entered our churches and stirred their quiet pools. Meetings crowd on meetings. The same energetic souls are found at them all, and engaged in many good works besides. But we must beware that we do not substitute in our own experience the active for the contemplative, the valley for the mountain-top. Neither can with safety be divorced from the other. The sheep must go in and out. The blood must come back to the heart to be recharged with oxygen before being impelled again to the extremities.

We must make time to be alone with God. The closet and the shut door are indispensable. We must lose the glare of the sunny piazza, that we may see the calm angel figures bending above the altar. We must escape the din of the world to become accustomed to the accents of the still small voice. Like David, we must sit before the Lord. Happy are they who have an observatory in their heart-house, to which they can often retire beneath the great arch of eternity, turning their telescope to the mighty constellations that burn beyond life's fever, and reaching regions where the breath of human applause or censure cannot follow.

It is only in such moments that the best spiritual gifts will loom on our vision, or we shall have grace to receive them. It is impossible to rush into God's presence, catch up anything we fancy, and run off with it. To attempt this will end in mere delusion and disappointment. Nature will not unveil her rarest beauty to the chance tourist. Pictures which are the result of a life of work do not disclose their secret loveliness to the saunterer down a gallery. No character can be read at a glance. And God's best cannot be ours apart from patient waiting in His holy presence. The superficial may be put off with a parable, a pretty story, but it is not given such to know the mysteries of the kingdom of heaven.

2. *We must be possessed by an eager desire.* There is a difference between wishing for a thing and willing it. We pass a shop-window filled with choice and expensive articles, and say lightly, "I should like to have this or the other." But the mere wish does not suffice to give us what we like, because it is not strong enough to induce us to part with our money to obtain it. In a single afternoon we wish for a hundred differing objects, and forget them all within an hour. But how different to this is the fixed determination, the settled purpose, of the *will!* The lad catches sight of some equipment for his

sport, the student of a precious book, the lover of a rare and jeweled ornament which he covets for the one he loves. In each case the will is wrought upon till it resolves to acquire at any cost. Then privation and self-sacrifice and delay are cheerfully encountered. Nothing can extinguish or slacken the determination that follows hard after its quest. So with us. We must hunger and thirst; we must be possessed by strong and passionate desire; we must be resolved to use even violence to take the kingdom of heaven. The expressions of Scripture are all so intense: the hart pants for the waterbrooks; Jacob will not let the angel go; the widow troubles the unjust judge day and night. We too shall have this strong desire if we will let the Spirit of God produce it within our hearts. But the merchantman must be bent on seeking and finding the goodly pearl. We must strive to enter the strait gate. We must agonize, to use the apostle's word, as the athlete for the crown.

3. *We must have a promise in our hand.* This is the true method of dealing with God. Search the Bible for some holy word which exactly fits your case. It will not be hard to find one, since it abounds with personal incidents culled from every conceivable variety of life. Then, when it has been discovered, and perhaps borne in on you by the

divine Spirit, take it with you into the presence of God, or place your finger upon it as you pass into the presence-chamber with hushed and reverent step. Every place which the sole of your foot shall tread shall be yours; such was the olden promise. And its counterpart is realized when we can put our foot down on some definite word of God and reverently say, "I ask that Thou wouldest fulfil this for me. Do as Thou hast said. Give me the portion of goods that falleth to me. Let me know all Thy meaning hidden here."

All spiritual things are ours in Jesus, but they are only revealed to us one by one as we need. Our need is intended to make us look up for and claim the blessing intended to meet it; and the promise is God's invitation to come to God for it.

4. *Reckon on God.* If you desire spiritual gifts, not for your own gratification, but for the glory of Christ; if, so far as you know, your heart is rid of evil and your life of sinful habit; if you perceive that the promise is for you, because you are not only a son, but an heir of God and a joint heir with Christ; if you feel an eager desire that God has instilled to lead you to this very point—*then* open your mouth wide and believe that God fills it; unshutter every window and believe that the light enters; throw wide every aper-

ture and believe that you have received what you needed and sought. According to your faith it shall be unto you. What you have been able to take by faith, that you count upon. You may not have the emotion you expected, nor the sense of blessing you looked for, but you will have God, God's gift, God's answer to your faith. And you may go your way and reckon that you have what you sought. Then in some moment of need, or when you least expect it, or when engaged in wonted toils, some glad consciousness of joy or peace, or nearness to Christ, or power over others will be the evidence that you did receive.

XIV

OUR EQUABLENESS

"Continue in prayer, and watch."—COL. IV. 2.

THERE are many among us who are either very *up* or very *down*. The pendulum of their life is always swinging up to its extreme height or down to its extreme depth. They are either standing on the crest of the mountain, intoxicated with the exhilarating air, or they are lost in the deep ravine, where the sunshine hardly penetrates through the overhanging branches. They are not the happiest temperaments to live with. On the whole, give me for traveling a good level road, at a moderate elevation, and I will gladly dispense with the succession of ascents, each of which is followed by its descent.

There is another class of people who are excessively amiable and pleasant to you to-day, but when you meet them to-morrow they are as cold and distant as possible. These are creatures of moods and tenses. They resemble the month of March, which may be warm and beautiful or as piercing with shafts of cold. To be friends with such people is to expose one's self to constant unrest. You never know how you will find them, and must always go into their society provided with a coat and umbrella in case of storms.

There is yet another class, who are sometimes on fire for God and the souls of men, burning with clear and ardent flame, before which other souls stand deeply rebuked. We say instinctively, "Who are these which are arrayed in these dazzling garments, and whence came they?" But after a few weeks the fire dies down, the enthusiasm cools. They do not pray with the same fervor; they have given up their buttonholing of strangers and their entreaties to their friends; they have renounced the system of Bible study which they took up with such zest; they are absent from the class and service into which they plunged with so much vigor. They remind one of the paper and chips which the express-train catches up in its rush, but which, after eddying for a little in its wake, drop down again to silence and neglect till the next rushes by.

On all these might be written the inscription which the dying Jacob engraved upon the life of Reuben: "Unstable as water, thou shalt not excel" (Gen. xlix. 4).

Some of this comes from undue excitement

and unnatural overstrain. We travel at such a speed, there must be moments of reaction when the nervous system rebounds. We live so near the limits of our strength that we have none to draw upon in hours of crisis, and have to make demands on our reserve which seriously tax our powers of recuperation. We do more and attempt more than we have power for. Moreover, we fail to allow for the great influence of our nervous system on our emotional life, or to distinguish between our emotions and our will.

There is no doubt that overstrain soon affects the nervous tissues, and these immediately register their condition on the emotions. The prophet, exhausted by the demands of Carmel, asks that he may die; the Baptist, shut up in the prison walls from the free, glad air, doubts whether Jesus be the Christ. Under the impulse of inspiring oratory and the excitement of vast crowds we greatly resolve and greatly begin; but when these have passed our pace diminishes till we come to a stand. We allow ourselves to be drawn in a certain direction by impulse rather than by principle, by our attraction to people rather than by the thought of how we may serve them; and then after a while we lose our interest in them and look at them with a cold and critical eye.

Young people, it is of the utmost importance that you should watch against this unequableness. Do not be like feather-down floating in the air, or the flotsam or jetsam carried to and fro on the face of the tide. Guard against fickleness. There are several safeguards and preventives.

Cultivate strong habits of right thinking and right doing. Oh for trumpet tones to make all the young people of our time take heed! In after life it is of immense help for living highly and nobly to have the assistance of habit—not simply to do a right thing because you are impelled to it, but because such is your habit; not to read your chapter for a few mornings because you have been to a consecration meeting or a convention, but because it has become your habit from childhood to do so; not to act courteously and pleasantly because you have freshly come from the sunshine and air of some lovely environment, but because you have made it the habit of your life to be a true knight of the cross—chivalrous, courteous, self-forgetting, thoughtful of the yearnings of other souls for sympathy and help in life's rough way; and not to do your Christian service under a spasm of interest wrought in you by the suggestion of another or a passing pity, but because your Master, Christ, has laid it on you as a solemn duty to Himself.

We build up such habits by single actions,

and especially in the earlier part of our lives. If only young people would take themselves in hand and concentrate thought on the well-doing of each single act of their early years, they would find habits forming around them, strong and enduring as iron, which would greatly help them after in moments of strain and stress. Even to form such a habit as early rising, and persistently watching each morning hour, and insisting on obedience to the whirr of the alarm, will be of immense importance in after life. What is difficult at first becomes in time a second nature and a permanent acquisition to the furniture of the soul.

It would be well to fix the following saying by an eminent writer deeply in the soul:

> " Sow a thought, you reap an act;
> Sow an act, you reap a habit;
> Sow a habit, you reap a character;
> Sow a character, you reap a destiny."

Live in your standing in Christ Jesus. Quoting from my own experience, I have found this of priceless worth. In fact, when a friend asked me recently whether I did not suffer from fits of depression as a natural reaction from strenuous effort, I instantly reminded him that one might be very sensitive to such a nervous rebound and yet guard against its injuring or depressing the spiritual life, first by attributing it to its right cause, and next by remembering that no depression of the nervous system can affect our standing in Jesus, which is altogether apart from ourselves and altogether determined by what He has done and is.

You may be tired and unnerved, unable to feel as you are wont, below par, and out of sorts; all around you may be depressing and difficult; a morbid wish to be quit of it all may haunt you; a sense that God is dealing hardly with you may stay the song of your soul; but remember that you are yet His child; that in Jesus you are accepted and beloved; that your place is beside Him in the heavenlies. Rise, my heart; thou art the child of the great King; thy life is hidden with Christ in God; thine are the illimitable ages. All this is true, however thou feelest.

Find compensation in God. If sad, find rest and peace in Him; if down and depressed, claim His joy; if glad and buoyant, seek His lowliness and meekness. If wanting in earnestness, ask His good Spirit to quicken you; if too exuberant, ask Him to calm you. If standing high on the mount, ask that you may walk with Him in your high places. If attracted to people, ask that He may ratify the friendship, always keeping it in Himself; if repelled, seek that you may love them with His love. Let the nature and love of God be the makeweight and compensation for all that is dark and sad or evil in yourself and your surroundings. "Why art thou cast down, O my soul? and why art thou disquieted within me? hope thou in God."

Exercise a strong self-restraint. Never have mercy on yourself, or excuse any deflection from your own high ideal. Be harder on yourself than your grimmest critic. Never say that weariness or depression or heartsickness can excuse anything which is not perfectly lovely and of good report. Put on the Lord Jesus Christ and wear His image ever. Trust the Holy Spirit to make His presence ever more real and absorbing.

XV

UNSPOTTED

" Unspotted from the world."—JAMES I. 27.

THERE are many definitions of religion. Some say that it is right thinking, others that it is right feeling; but James strikes through these and says that the core of real religion is unspottedness (James i. 27).

The world is a very filthy place. We cannot walk along its causeways without the risk of being bespattered from head to foot. A sea of ink splashes up against our homes and sends its tides up into drawing-rooms and kitchens, churches and schools, and it is very hard to avoid its drenching spray. Only a few elect souls are able to keep themselves unspotted from the world. Yet it is possible. The Lord Jesus was a Lamb without blemish and without spot. He offered Himself unto God without spot, through the eternal Spirit, and He is able to keep us from stumbling and present us without spot before the presence of His glory with exceeding joy. Oh that we may all experience His keeping grace and be at last included in the bride which He shall present to Himself, glorious, without blemish and without spot!

It is a very attractive figure. Untrodden snow, like that which lies for miles over the high Alps, the lily with its untarnished calyx, the white surplice of the chorister lad, the sheen of the silver moonlight, the purity of white heat, the transparency of light, the flesh of a babe, are very attractive to us. Probably there is no story from the Old Testament more fascinating in interest than that which tells how the leprous flesh of the old warrior Naaman became pure as that of a little child, and no text more precious, because more suggestive of unsullied purity, than that which declares that though sins be as scarlet they may be as white as snow, and though they be red like crimson they may be as wool.

Why is this, except that we feel so far away from our ideal and find some satisfaction in admiring it from afar? Perhaps there is something in each of us which instinctively craves kinship with unspottedness. We dimly remember our high origin, and mourn our loss of the stamp and hall-mark of purity with which God impressed us when Adam passed from His molding hand in paradise. We are attracted by that for which we were created and have lost. It has a divine fascination for sin-weary hearts. How delightful the snow-clad peaks of the Himalayas appear to the dwellers on the scorching plains of India!

But unspottedness is as necessary as it is attractive. God cannot use us if we are indifferent to the claims of purity and careless whether we are spotted or not. He is so strict that He bids us hate the very garment which is spotted with the flesh. "Be ye clean, ye that bear the vessels of the Lord."

He is so holy that He cannot unveil His rarest love to those who lack sensitiveness in regard to their walk through the world. We are told that only the pure in heart can see God. Nothing can surpass His tender mercy for those who have fallen and become blemished and spotted through weakness, ignorance, and passion; but nothing can compensate for a thoughtless, careless, worldly life, in which the soul shows no anxiety to keep itself unspotted.

The life of heaven down here, and the heaven that is yet to be, are alike impossible save to those who, so far as they know, endeavor to keep themselves unspotted. "This ye know of a surety, that no fornicator, nor unclean person, . . . hath any inheritance in the kingdom of Christ and God." Would you have God come to make His mansion with you? You must cleanse yourself from all filthiness of the flesh and spirit. Would you go at last to make your mansion with God? You must wash your robe and make it white in the blood of the Lamb. Only those who wash their robes have any right to the tree of life and to enter in through the gates into the city (Rev. xxii. 14, R. V.).

But it seems an impossible, impracticable dream. The lives of the greatest saints are entitled "Confessions." Every one in turn takes the bow and aims the arrow at the target, but is compelled to acknowledge failure. One only, born of woman, ever hit the silver center of absolute unspottedness; all else must appropriate the acknowledgment, "I have sinned, and perverted that which was right, and it has not profited." Job said he was vile; Isaiah, that his lips were unclean; Peter, that he was a sinful man; John, that for a man to say that he had not sinned was to be self-deceived. In such a world, with such a nature, opposed by such an adversary, how can we hope to be unspotted? And even if we are unspotted before men, what are we before the sight of God, to whom the heavens are not clean?

But God waits to assist us. We cannot help having a nature keenly susceptible to evil; we cannot avoid being tempted. The Evil One will knock at the door, and even shout his unhallowed suggestions through the keyhole. The world and society are no friends to grace; the newspapers are spotted with divorce-court and other items; the current novels are spotted with suggestive scenes and allusions; the streets are filled with spotted men and women; the shop-windows are littered with spotted photographs. But God is stronger and greater than all. He would not command what He cannot help us to realize. It is clear that by His loving grace we may so live as to win the beatitude of the unspotted. But we must use constantly the blood, the water, and the fire.

1. *The blood of Jesus.* It cleanseth from all sin. If the blood of bulls and goats and the ashes of an heifer sprinkling the unclean availed, under the old law, for the purifying of the flesh, how much more shall the blood of Christ cleanse our consciences and make us without spot before Him in love! Directly we confess our sins all the evil stains which have been contracted vanish utterly and forever. The microscope can detect blood-marks in linen which has been washed, but no magnifying power can ever discover sin which has been once confessed and put away. "It may be sought for, but it shall not be found." You may confess other sins if you will, but never that. God will remem-

ber it no more. You may remember it to humble you, but not to confess.

2. *The Word of God is compared to water.* Christ cleanses His church through the Word, as in a laver of water. Depend on it that there is no better method of a young man cleansing his way than by taking heed thereto according to God's Word. We read the Bible for purposes of a truer knowledge of God and His ways and for spiritual quickening; but let us use it more frequently as the bath of the spirit; let us bathe in it; let us revel in it as the grimy children of the slums in the laughing wavelets of river and sea.

3. *The fire of the Holy Spirit.* If you will hand over to Him your thoughts He will run them through a sieve of flame, burning out the germs of evil and allowing only the pure, natural, and guileless to pass. There is no such preservative against the germs of disease as fire. Ask the Holy Spirit to be within you as fire consuming the evil. Seek to live with the devouring fire and to dwell in the everlasting burnings of God's most holy and loving nature. Never leave your chamber in the morning without putting on the armor of light which is woven of flame, and be sure that, though spots may alight, they cannot remain amid its intense heat.

The unspotted are most tender and merciful to the spotted. They at least dare not draw their garments around them and shake themselves free of defiling contact. They know too well the perils from which they have been rescued and their own weakness, and they are merciful.

XVI

USE YOUR SENSES

"To discern both good and evil."—HEB. v. 14.

THE five senses of the body have their correlatives in the soul. From earliest childhood we naturally use the outward; the eye, ear, nose, mouth, and sense of touch are under constant requisition. But there are thousands of Christians in whom the senses of the soul are dormant and useless. They have eyes, but they see not; ears, but they hear not; mouths that do not taste, and hands that cannot feel. And it is for this reason that they always remain in the babe condition, needing to be fed by spoon and to be wheeled about in a perambulator.

The great use of ministers, to many people, is to serve as nurses, perpetually feeding, carrying, soothing, or supplying with sweetmeats and comfort.

If we are ever to grow out of the babe into the mature state we must learn by reason of use to exercise our senses to discern good and evil (Heb. v. 14).

Let us take the senses of the soul in order:

THE SENSE OF SMELL.—The wholesomeness or otherwise of natural objects is largely indicated by their odors. What is fragrant is for the most part wholesome, what is noisome, deleterious to health. We ought to be very thankful for the bad smells in the world where they indicate the presence of corruption and death. They have been arranged by a divine Providence in order to warn us away from places and substances that would depress and imperil health. Imagine a world in which hurtful things were inodorous or attractive in their scent! In how many cases should we be lured to ruin! God has labeled hurtful things "Poison" by their deterrent and noxious odors, which repel us as far from them as possible.

The nose, therefore, preserves us from many an unseen danger. It is a great privation to be without the sense of smell. Its loss is the forfeiture of one of the warning signals on the road of life. A quick scent enables one to escape from the neighborhood of disease-breeding spots. I had an illustration of this the other day. On my return from America I found my sense of smell greatly sharpened by the sea voyage, and was able to detect the presence of a sewage farm which had escaped the observation of my friends, securing for them as well as for myself immunity from the effects of undesirable contact with sewage matter. How often, too, a whiff of foul odor has made one turn immediately aside, hold the breath, and make for fresh air!

In the soul there is a similar power. God has endowed us with a marvelous sensitiveness to the presence of evil when it is yet at a distance. Before the evil thing has come within measurable distance of the soul, while it is only a whiff in the air, we may become aware of it and shelter in Jesus. One of the gifts of the Spirit is to make us quick of scent in the fear of the Lord, quick to detect the proximity of all that is inconsistent with the fear of God (Isa. xi. 3, marg.).

Let us ask for this sensitiveness; it will enable us to keep out of the way of temptation. With a shudder we shall escape, as Joseph did, from the room where the pestilence may lurk beneath silks or satins and the fragrance of eau de Cologne.

THE SENSE OF HEARING.—Solomon asked for an understanding (literally, a hearing) heart. Every musician knows the importance of a good ear. However fine the quality or strong the power of a voice, if the ear fails to detect the slightest dissonance with the pitch of the instrument, excellence as a singer is unattainable. To sing flat is bad enough, but to sing flat and not know it is unpardonable. You can do nothing with the unsensitive ear. On the other hand, you may train the ear to almost any degree of delicacy, so that it can appreciate shades of tone which are undiscoverable by ordinary listeners.

Do you not think that sins against charity committed by the tongue are due to a want of education and refinement in the ear of the soul? That singer would not sing flat if her ear were trained and quick. No, and that Christian would not be able to pass on those questionable stories, or retail those unkind statements, if his ear were trained to the cords of the heart of God.

We have met men to whom a discord was perfect agony. They have risen up and fled from a singer who was habitually out of tune. It is not so often that we meet men fleeing from speech which fell out with the deep music of heaven; but there are such. A little while ago, at Mr. Moody's table, I heard him interpose when one, in the course of conversation, in speaking of another, was a little below concert pitch. Oh that by reason of use we could exercise this sense!

THE SENSE OF SIGHT.—The apostle complains of people who were near-sighted and could not see afar off. It is a terrible affliction. Hagar's tears made her short-sighted, and she saw not the fountain of water. Elisha's servant was too near-sighted to see the horses and chariots of fire around him. Demas was too blind to look beyond the present evil world, and failed to see the unseen and eternal things that filled the vision of Paul.

But short-sightedness is not the main disease of the eyes. The Lord says that we may see double, as though we suffered from a squint. It is said that Edward Irving suffered from a squint which spoiled the front view of his face because as a baby he slept in a cot which had a large hole in its side, and he contracted the habit of looking through it as he lay. Whether that be so or not, there are plenty of professing Christians whose eyes do not move on the same axis; one is directed to heaven, the other to earth—one to God, the other to man. Such may well stumble in the noonday.

All along the path of life are stumbling-blocks and pitfalls which at any moment may involve us in terrible falls. Near-sightedness or obliqueness of vision is alike to be dreaded. Only when the eye is single can the whole body be full of light. But when "the light that is in thee is darkness, how great is the darkness!" And "he that walketh in darkness knoweth not whither he goeth." How eagerly do we need that Jesus should lay His hands on our eyes, that we may see all things clearly!

THE SENSE OF TASTE.—This too is a marvelous preservative of health and life. We can tell almost invariably what is good for food by the taste. Rotten fruit, diseased meat, uncanny tinned oysters, are immediately rejected by the palate as unfit to go farther into the body. It would seem as though a janitor sat at the gate of the digestive organs, carefully testing every substance as it passed, admitting or rejecting. We know well enough when food will nourish us.

So the soul has taste. Instantly it can distinguish wholesome from unwholesome words. It recognizes the Bible as being good and healthful food, sweeter than honey and the honeycomb. It detects the flavor of deity in the Bible, and this is the best proof of its inspiration. You may not be able to argue or define it, but you are aware of its presence in the Bible as nowhere else.

And whenever you are conscious that a story-book or a newspaper paragraph or a conversation is unwholesome, be sure to eject it as suddenly and forcibly as you may. Exercise this sense.

THE SENSE OF TOUCH.—Be very sensitive to the touch of Jesus. Very often He gives a touch, light as a feather, which is the signal that danger is near. Be warned by it. Harden not your heart.

Be equally sensitive to the touch of the weary and heavy-laden. They will come near you in the throng and press of life. Be on the alert for such, and stay to ask, as Jesus did, "Who touched Me?" Like Him, we should be easily touched by the feeling of men's infirmities.

But all these senses, like those of the body, will grow with use, becoming daily more delicate and sensitive, discerning between good and evil and causing us to develop from babyhood into maturity.

XVII

THE LIGHT OF THAT DAY

"When the day of Pentecost was fully come."—
ACTS II. I.

IF the story of Acts i. and ii. had been dropped out of the earliest manuscripts, and the book had begun with chapter iii., we should have been compelled to believe that some event of unparalleled interest and importance had occurred to account for the astounding alteration in Peter and the rest of the apostles from what we had seen them to be during the closing days of Christ's ministry and to the very slopes of the Ascension Mount.

You cannot have an effect without a cause, and without an adequate cause. If at one moment you see a train of carriages standing quietly on the rails, and in five minutes after you see them moving rapidly, you instantly infer the existence of a power, which was formerly quiescent, in active operation. So the contrast between Luke xxiv. and Acts iii.

demands such an explanation as is given us in Acts i. and ii. Let the mind of a thoughtful man be confronted with the church and account to us for the marvelous momentum she received at the time of Christ's ascension, and let it find a more adequate explanation, if it can, than that which is given in the story of the advent of the Holy Spirit to the little assembly in the upper room.

In Luke the disciples were too slow of heart to understand the Scriptures; in the earlier chapters of the Acts we are amazed at the multitude and variety of Scripture quotations and the unerring accuracy with which they are applied.

In Luke they tremble and flee before their Master's captors, and Peter especially plays the part of coward; but, behold, they stand firm as rocks and charge their judges with the murder of the Messiah.

In Luke they have bitter sorrow, half-hearted enthusiasm, little power with God or man; but in the Acts we read: "The multitude of them that believed were of one heart and soul. . . . And with great power gave the apostles witness of the resurrection of the Lord Jesus: and great grace was upon them all."

If only you would claim your share in the blessings which the day of Pentecost brought to them that were afar off (Gentiles) as well as to them that were near (Jews), and to all whom the Lord our God should call unto Him,—blessings which are as unexhausted as though none had ever made use of them, blessings which can be had from the Saviour on the one single condition of accepting and using them,—there would be for you also an immediate entrance on the enjoyment of those same privileges which fell to the share of the first disciples. Let us enumerate those priceless gains:

Insight into Scripture. Words spoken by the prophets, psalms written by the sweet singer, events in the story of the exodus, will flash with new meaning. The light of that day shall illumine many a dark chamber and intricate passage in the palace of Scripture. When the Spirit who spake in kings and prophets speaks within us, things which were hidden from the wise and prudent stand revealed to babes. Dark masses of truth, touched by the heavenly fire, yield back the light they caught ages ago from the face of God. The heart is open to understand the Scriptures; the eyes see with a divine insight. Old chapters seen in the fresh light assume new interest, trivial incidents a new importance, historical events a deeper meaning. The Holy Spirit, like a good householder, brings from the storehouse of Scripture things new and old. As He speaks with us our hearts burn, and, to our surprise, we find the miracle of the transfiguration repeated and the common texture of Holy Writ is radiant with the glory of God.

Great boldness of utterance. A little while ago you trembled like an aspen-leaf before the question of a maid, but when that day breaks you stand like a lion and are able to charge men with their sin—no hesitancy in speech, no cringing in demeanor, no quailing of the fearless eye. "Him, being delivered by the determinate wisdom and foreknowledge of God, ye have taken, and by wicked hands did crucify and slay"—such is our challenge. "Him hath God exalted by His right hand to be a Prince and a Saviour"—such our unhesitating announcement.

Have you reached this stage of holy boldness, so that at your rebuke the wicked man is arrested, the attention of the careless compelled, and the ungodly pricked to the heart? Then be sure that that day has broken. If it be otherwise your day of Pentecost has not fully come.

Much joy. You may have lost the sensible presence of your dearest friend. Only ten days ago you may have seen him ascend to God; you may have returned to an upper room, every timber in which recalls the presence which has been withdrawn; but when that day has fully come you will be filled with such ecstasy of love and joy and hope as to excite wonder in bystanders. It will be exhilaration like that of a man filled with new wine. You will take your food with gladness and singleness of heart, praising God; you will speak in psalms and hymns and spiritual songs, singing and making melody with your heart to the Lord, giving thanks always for all things, in the name of our Lord Jesus Christ, to God, even the Father.

Burning love. Recently I stood by the mouth of a furnace of molten metal prepared for pouring into the mold of a large cylinder. What a contrast between the liquid metal, that dazzled and turned away the gaze, and the dark sand of the mold! But presently the sluice-gate was opened and the stream of fire began to pour into its prepared bed, and speedily every corner and cranny far beneath my feet had received its infilling. And as I stood above it I loved to think of that mold of fire. This is Pentecost! For years Jesus had been making the mold in the hearts of the disciples, but when He left them it was little more than an empty void—capacious, hungry, but empty. When the day of Pentecost came He drew back the sluice-gates, and the Holy Spirit, like the liquid fire of the metal, poured into hearts and lives which were prepared and eager.

What that day was to the disciples it is to

every one. Before there may be orthodoxy of creed, punctilious regularity in the performance of religious duty, correctness in behavior and speech, but that is all. Wait till that day breaks, and that God, who is fire and strength and purity and, above all, love, fills heart and life. Then the love of God is shed abroad by the Holy Ghost, and the love wherewith the Father loved the Son is in us, and He is in us, according to His high-priestly prayer.

Power with God and man. See those crowds swaying beneath Peter's simple words! You cannot account for the effect by what he said. Half his address was quotation. He told the story of Calvary, which they knew, and of the resurrection, which was startling and strange. He dilated on the ascension and his Master's reception of the Holy Spirit. There was nothing in what he said to account for the marvelous result of three thousand being added to the Lord. The only explanation of the marvel was that he had been with God, that the day of Pentecost had fully come, and that the power of God Himself was pouring through the open flood-gates of his soul. Such power is within your reach if you would only go forth and stand in the meridian light of the day of Pentecost.

Of that day Christ is the day-star. The

Latins called the morning star Lucifer, because it seemed to bring the day. Jesus is the bright and morning star; He has received the Holy Spirit from the Father, that He may communicate Him to all who are united with Him by a living faith. Deal with Him; ask Him to shed this blessed gift upon you; receive it by faith and reckon that it is yours; be sure that the day has broken, even though you have detected no footfall of its stealthy entrance. You undoubtedly received the Spirit at regeneration, else you had not been able to call Christ "Lord"; but there is something more to be had, as much better than this as sunlight is than starlight—the full coming of the day of Pentecost.

XVIII

THE SECRET OF CONTINUANCE

"Daniel continued."—DAN. I. 21.

THE closing words of the first chapter of the Book of Daniel are very significant. We are told that "Daniel *continued* even unto the first year of Cyrus." If he were about fourteen years of age at the time of his transportation this would mean that for seventy additional years he continued to practise those habits of self-control and abstinence which he had commenced in his youth. "Simple words, but what a volume of tried faithfulness is involved by them! Amid all the intrigues indigenous at all times to dynasties of Oriental despotism; amid all the envy toward a foreign captive in high office as a king's counselor; amid all the trouble incidental to the insanity of the king and the murder of two of his successors—in that whole critical period for his people Daniel *continued*."

Not unfrequently young souls are deterred

from confessing Christ, or assuming some pledge of lofty endeavor and entire surrender, for fear that they may prove recreant to their high resolve. This may seem to betoken modesty of disposition and a low self-estimate; but much more certainly it betokens mistrust of God and unworthy conceptions of His love and power—as though it were possible for Him to excite yearnings and aspirations which He could not satisfy, or begin a work which He was unable to perfect! Our duty and privilege is to obey, and to step out into the unknown believing that He who gave the command will supply all needed grace for its execution, and will never suffer the righteous to be ashamed.

Our sources of continuance are furnished by the offices of the distinct persons of the blessed Trinity.

First, in the purpose of the Father. There are hours in life when it is of the greatest possible comfort to get down to the bed-rock of His electing grace. This doctrine ought not to be presented to the inquirer, for, whatever it may mean, it contains nothing to discourage the free access of any and every one to God. He has not spoken in secret and said of any seeking soul, "Seek ye My face in vain." Nay, for all the world the door of mercy stands open, and over it this legend is inscribed: "Whosoever will, let him enter.

THE SECRET OF CONTINUANCE

... Him that cometh to Me I will in no wise cast out." It is only when we have entered that ever-open door that we are confronted with another legend, inscribed in gold and set around the room: "In whom also we were made a heritage, having been foreordained according to the purpose of Him who worketh all things after the counsel of His own will." In other words, the comfort and meaning of God's electing purpose is not for those who are *without*, but for such as are *within*, God's home.

There is a verse which casts a little light into the mysterious depths of this truth—not very far, but for some few feet: that from which we learn that whom God did foreknow He also did predestinate; as though His divine wisdom forecasted those who should become one with Jesus by a living faith, and His divine purpose included them in its unchanging determinations.

Do you not feel the force of these thoughts? Do you not see their immense reassurance? Is it not a comfort, when the hatred of Satan is like a pitiless hail-storm in your face, to believe that the love of God will never let you go? Is it not inspiring and helpful to realize, when you are most inclined to despond, that there is no fickleness, vacillation, or changefulness in the divine heart? He knew all we should be before He loved us.

He knew all the difficulties of making us saints before He excavated us from nature's quarry. We did not choose Him, but He us. We did not first love Him, but He us. However strong the gale may be against us, our keel is in the strong current of His will, and this will master that. "My sheep shall never perish, neither shall any pluck them out of My hand. My Father, which gave them Me, is greater than all; and none shall pluck them out of My Father's hand."

Next, there is the constant supply of grace from the Saviour. The prophet saw in vision that the bowl of the temple candlestick was fed with golden oil from the heart of two olive-trees. These symbolize the king and priest sides of Christ's nature, and teach us that the oil of the divine grace is constantly ministered to us from his heart, and as long as that continues we shall continue. Because Jesus lives we shall live also.

This makes the difference between the old covenant and the new. God sorrowfully laments that His people continued not in His covenant; and then our attention is directed from the priests of the old covenant, who were not suffered to continue by reason of death, to Him who, because He continueth ever, hath an unchangeable priesthood and is able to save unto the uttermost all that come unto God by Him, seeing that

THE SECRET OF CONTINUANCE 119

He ever liveth to make intercession for them (Heb. vii. 24, 25; viii. 9). Your continuance and mine depend on the continuance of Jesus as our minister and mediator before the throne of God.

The other night I fell into converse with the wick of my oil lamp, that for many weeks has ministered light to me. Some grateful acknowledgment was made for silent, regular, and unobtrusive service, and then the question came whether it did not shrink from the inevitable demands of the long winter nights. I could see in the glass oil cistern in which the wick lay coiled together that there was a considerable length yet to run, and I knew that the scissors cut off each morning a very inconsiderable piece of char, and I said:

"In view of the great and inevitable demands of the future, does not your heart misgive you? How will you be able to last out, how continue to supply light for my page?"

And for my reply I got the following: "I do not produce the light; I only supply the edge or fringe on which the oil burns. From the cistern yonder it climbs up by me, as by a ladder, and burns on my extremity to give light to all that are in the house. As long as the oil is supplied, so that there is no lack, and as long as the charred edge is removed, so that there is nothing to choke the access of the oil to the flame, I most certainly shall continue."

Similarly, our continuance depends on the unceasing thought and care of Jesus. He walks amid the seven golden candlesticks. Whenever there is need for the golden snuffers He does not hesitate to use them, and while He lives there is no fear of failure in the holy oil. Out of His heart it ever pours to every believer, just as the oxygenated blood is poured forth throughout the entire body and to every part.

The mill-wheel never dreams of turning itself, and never anticipates ceasing in its useful ministry, because the stream is ever flowing beneath, and the miller lives at hand to obviate any, even the slightest, symptom of failure.

Lastly, there is the perpetual indwelling of the Holy Spirit. He does not say yea and nay—one thing to-day and another to-morrow. The life He communicates is everlasting, since it is eternal; and it is eternal because He gives Himself as the eternal Spirit. The eternal is not subject to decay or change or evanescence. It persists. Our hope cannot make us ashamed, because the love of God is shed abroad in our heart; and what is this but the Shechinah, the nature of the "I AM," who was manifested in the bush that burned with fire, the tender branchlets of which were not consumed because they were not required to yield fuel to the flame!

Rejoice, O trembling heart! The Holy Spirit has come to indwell thee, and He will not leave His residence. He has chosen thee as His temple, and He will not be driven forth. He has given thee glimpses, yearnings, first-fruits, which are the earnest of an inheritance that He cannot do otherwise than grant. He has begun a good work, and will carry it on to the day of Jesus Christ. There are no unfinished pictures in His gallery, no unperfected blocks in His studio. "The work which His grace has begun the arm of His strength will complete."

XIX

ONE OF GOD'S "NOES"

"I had in mine heart to build a house."— 1 CHRON. XXVIII. 2, 3.

"As for me, I had in mine heart to build a house of rest for the ark of the covenant of the Lord." Thus spake the aged king, and it was a true record. For scarcely had the outbursts of loyalty which greeted him to the throne died away than he began to plan for the building of a house which should be more worthy of the God he loved than the faded curtains of the tabernacle, stained with the travel and wear of centuries. Was not this very remarkable? He had spent his life among wild outlaws, roughing it on the hills and in caves, familiar with war and bloodshed, and with fierce men as his comrades. He had shed much blood, and one would not have expected him to be so sensitive to the impulse of a noble purpose, or that his soul would have been kept so full of sweetness, only awaiting a fitting occasion for its expression. Yet there it was. Though he was kept so long at rough, distasteful work, he never lost this tender, holy longing to build a house of rest. And ere he died he took forth once more the ideal of his life, and looked at it wistfully for the last time ere he laid it aside forever.

So it is still. Many around us who are doing rough and uncongenial work carry within them a fair ideal of some great and lovely thing which they would fain achieve. Some dream of music fills the chambers of harmony. Some vision of golden glory is painted with rich, prismatic colors on the windows of the soul. Some scheme of far-reaching benevolence and consecrated service exercises the sleeping and waking thoughts and keeps the fountains of the heart always pure.

They will yet be missionaries. They will stir men to noble ideals. They will build houses of rest for the weary and heavy laden. They will start fountains flowing which shall carry refreshment far down into the valleys where the toiling myriads stifle. And as God looks down on them He says with a smile, "It is well that this is in thine heart." It is well to have such heavenly occupants —well because when the heart is occupied thus worse things are compelled to wait without; well because the pure in heart are blessed; well because a noble purpose is the parent, here and hereafter, of a noble progeny (1 Kings viii. 18).

At first when Nathan heard the royal suggestion he welcomed it as the best thing possible. Neither he nor David dreamed for a moment that God would say "No." Yet so it was. We cannot judge God's way for one another. Like Peter and John, we must learn to say, "Lord, and what shall this man do?" Because things which have seemed the best course possible to our poor human judgment are put aside by the wise love of God. In the morning the prophet had to seek his lord and tell him as gently as possible that it could not be.

God spoke His " No" very gently. Indeed, it was so wrapped up in promises of the coming child that the "No" was rather breathed than spoken, rather felt than heard. God always says "No" thus, so as not to break the bruised reed nor quench the smoking flax, so as not to break the heart of the most timid. If He is not able to remove the thorn in the flesh He says, "My grace is sufficient," and we are left to infer that our request cannot be granted.

God did not at first give any reason. Only after the lapse of years was the real reason borne in upon the spirit of the king, and he was taught that his disappointment was not due to arbitrary caprice, but because there was an incongruity between his project and his previous wars. God does not give His reasons at the time. He says, "Wait, My child, and trust Me; what thou knowest not now thou shalt know hereafter. I will tell thee My reason by and by." Then, after the years have passed, the true reason is suggested by a word, a circumstance, an impression, a flash of inspiration.

God sweetly wove His commendation with His " No." How grateful it must have been to David to hear God review his life-purpose and say that it was well conceived! Those words must have often recurred to him and been as the tree that sweetened the bitter waters of the brackish desert pools. All through life God may hinder us from executing the one purpose on which our hearts were set. There are the demands of home and dear ones, the limitation of our ability, the shackling fetters of circumstances. But at the close and end of all He will let us know that He detected our high purpose and was satisfied. The woman who welcomed the prophet for his Master's sake shall have an identical reward with his. Will it not repay us for years of deferred hope and delayed achievement when God says to us, " I saw it all; not one pang of pain or throb of desire was unrecognized or unappreciated;

I am pleased and satisfied; enter into My joy"?

Though God said " No" in one form, yet He fulfilled David's purpose in its noblest intention. The house was built mainly through David's means, his influence and provision and prayers. As the noble temple stood complete and radiant in the sunlight David's name passed from lip to lip; he was remembered, and all his afflictions. It was recorded how he sware to the Lord, and vowed to the mighty God of Jacob, that he would not give sleep to his eyes, nor slumber to his eyelids, till he had found a place for the Lord, an habitation for the mighty God of Jacob. And as David looked down from heaven he was content. Is your life-purpose balked and thwarted? Do your cherished plans miscarry? This were an insoluble problem if we did not believe that there is a world where the broken purposes of earth are realized on a wider and better scale than we once dared to hope.

And how patiently David bore himself under this rebuff! He was an Eastern tyrant, accustomed to be instantly obeyed; but he bore the frustrating of his life's purpose gently and submissively as a child. He did not turn his face to the wall in a pet. He did not sulk. He did not throw down his tools and refuse to do anything because he could not do the thing that he liked best. He said in effect, "It is the Lord; let Him do what seemeth Him good." And then he quietly set to work to do the next best thing in accumulating the ample stores which Solomon found ready to his hand and which made his work comparatively light.

This patience is one of the rarest virtues. We are so apt to fret and fume and strike work if God crosses our plans or seems to deny our request. Would that we could take God's lessons with loving fortitude! Would that we could suit ourselves to His mold of circumstances! Would that we could accept the inferior work if we may not take the higher!

> "Content to fill a little space,
> If He be glorified."

Some may be suffering now from the almost stunning blow of one of God's "Noes." It seems just now as though life were impossible and death a sweet release. Be strong, O heart, to suffer and wait! Begin to do some other work for God. The load may seem heavy at the outset, but it will become lighter at every step, and ere long the uncongenial road will open into unimagined beauties.

Yes, compensations will come—in having vindicated God's character, in being owned His child, and in hearing Him say, "Thou didst well in that it was in thine heart."

We know not what we are doing. When we are stopped in one direction we are gathering force in another. Kingdoms are won by waiting as well as by fighting. John speaks of "the kingdom and patience of Jesus."

XX

FORGETTING

"Forgetting those things which are behind."—
PHIL. III. 13.

THERE are some things which we must never forget. We are bidden to remember the way in which the Lord our God has led us; the wicket-gate where we passed from darkness to light; the cross where our burden rolled away; the night we spent in the House Beautiful. But He who bids us remember these things bids us forget others. We are to forget the things that are behind, and reach forward to those which are before, and so press toward the goal.

Very solemnly, in the midst of one of His discourses, our Lord bade His hearers remember Lot's wife. And why should they have been so specially exhorted to consider that pillar of salt standing in awful desolation on the plain of the Dead Sea? Why not think rather of Lot escaping in mad haste, or of the angels hastening him, or of the doom that overtook the sinners of Sodom? Ah, there are lessons that deserve pondering to be learned from that monument of basalt. "She looked back"—she squandered priceless moments, given for escape, in retrospect. Instead of pressing to the possibilities of a better future, she lingered regretfully over the relics of a disgraceful past. She is forever a type and a warning to those who fail to forget the things that are behind.

Forget past sins. There is a sense in which we do well to remember the past misdoings of our lives—that we may be humbled and warned; that we may not expose ourselves to temptations which have shown themselves too strong for us; that we may be led to a more careful self-watch and more entire dependence upon God. But we ought not to dwell upon our past sins as though they were ever present to the eye of God and incapacitated us for high and holy service.

What would Peter have done on the day of Pentecost if he had persisted in pensively dwelling on the scenes of the denial and had not dared to believe that all was forgiven and forgotten? What would have been the effect on the great apostle if he had allowed the memory of his share in the harrying of the saints to overcast his spirit when summoned to found churches, write epistles, and traverse continents? When once we confess it our sin is immediately and forever put away. God will never mention it again. It need not be a barrier on our service; it should not hinder us from aspiring to and enjoying the most intimate fellowship which is within the reach of mortals. Forget the past sins and failures of your life in the sense of brooding over them with perpetual lamentation.

Forget past successes. This is a very fruitful source of weakness. We are apt to suppose that we have reached the limit of our measure on some august occasion, over which we ponder with much self-congratulation. Thus we did and said and triumphed. Together with this, and following it swiftly, as tears do laughter, the thought flashes across the soul, " But I shall never do as well again; my sun has passed its meridian; my hand is losing its dexterity and cunning; my eye is not so keen, nor my foot as swift."

This will never do. Such thoughts may hold good in respect of the force of the mind and the muscle of the arm, but not of the spirit, which has the element of immortality in its constitution and does not share the failure of nature. "Thy sun shall no more go down, nor thy moon withdraw herself"; "more and more unto the perfect day"; "bearing fruit in old age"—such are the metaphors of Scripture. Dare to believe that there are greater and better things before than behind, that there are mightier victories, larger spoils, greater accomplishments. It would be a hundred pities if your memory of the past should be a ring-fence and stay your future development. Our future is not to be measured by more or less of natural vigor or intellectual faculty,—these may wax or wane,—but by the expansion of our spiritual character, the increase of faith, hope, and love, which ever abide, the capacity of our spirits to take in more and more of the fullness of God.

Forget past innocence. An innocent child is an engaging sight—the heart not polluted, the eyes not blurred with passion, the breath pure as a spring morning, the body a meet shrine for holy love. We contrast such with ourselves, who have eaten of the tree of knowledge of good and evil, and sadly say with Hood:

" I am further off from heaven to-day than when I was a boy."

But we should remember that purity, which knows evil and has triumphed over it, is a greater thing than innocence, just as the ship that has weathered storm and battle is a nobler object than the gay pleasure-boat on the eve of a regatta. To know sin only to hate it, to know it and to shrink from it as the timid gazelle from the beast of prey, to know it in order to warn others against it, is to resemble the Lamb of God, who was holy, harmless, undefiled, and separate from sinners. Do not, then, mourn over the tender grace of the morning; press on toward the noon, which, notwithstanding all its dust and glare, is ripening millions of ears of corn. Only be sure that if you have lost your innocence it has been replaced by purity. There are so many who have neither the one nor the other. But purity awaits all who will open their hearts to receive the indwelling grace and power of the Holy Spirit.

Forget past disappointments. Some always bear themselves as though they would say, " I am one who has seen affliction; call me Naomi, but call me Mara, for the Lord hath dealt very bitterly with me." There is a pensive, dejected look, as though God had forgotten to be gracious and had shut up His mercy forevermore. This does not commend our God to others, and it betrays a wrong state of things in ourselves. God can increase our capacity as the years go by, and our success does not depend on our natural powers or capacities, but on the ever-growing fullness of power and grace of which God is the fountain and character the recipient. If a father chastens a child we do not expect it to wear always after a downcast look. If it did we might fear that it had not forgiven its parent and were resenting the chastening as a personal wrong. The stripes should be accepted and pondered, but the face should be lightened again with the assurance of the father's forgiveness and perfect trust that all was lovingly meant.

So with ourselves. We may be as yet in young life, but we have seen sorrow; the shadow has passed over our sun, the sirocco has withered the green oasis on which we had thought to settle for the remainder of our days. Be it so. We can never forget the dear one taken from our side. But beside the cross there are springs of joy; let us drink of them. Much is gone, but, thank God, much is left. Let us look not only on our losses, but on our possessions. Let us lift to Him a face wet with tears, perhaps, yet full of love and trust, until He shall illumine it with the light of His countenance.

XXI

STAY WHERE YOU ARE

"Let every man abide in the same calling wherein he was called."—1 COR. VII. 20.

WHEN the apostle wrote his first epistle to Corinth the church there was full of unrest. The inspiration of a new life was breathing through the world like the warm breath of spring among icebergs, those natural temples of the far north, and beneath its touch venerable structures that had withstood centuries of violence showed signs of disintegration. The tyranny of man over woman was doomed when it appeared that in Christ there was no distinction between male and female, but that the salvation of a woman's soul was as precious to Him and cost as much as that of a man. The great Jewish system of temple, priesthood, and sacrifice was doomed when it was realized that approach to God might be direct and without the mediation of priest or the offering of sacrifice. The iniquitous slavery which accounted men as chattels, and prevailed in the most degrading form, was doomed when it was recognized that the slave had rights which no purchase-money could cancel, that he was his master's equal in the sight of God, and that the one standard before the eternal throne was character.

Times of transition are apt to breed a license of individual action which is mistaken for liberty. It was so in the French Revolution that closed the last century, and there are clear signs that the same tendency is asserting itself amid that momentous revolution through which the present century is coming to its close. Not otherwise was it when Paul wrote his letters to Corinth and to other churches. The ancient landmarks were being removed and the bands of society slackened. What wonder, then, that men thought the time had come for escaping from every yoke that chafed, from every burden that galled? There was a strong tendency to hold the marriage tie lightly, to attempt abrupt and revolutionary changes in church relations, and, above all, to anticipate the result of those social changes which were slowly taking shape. Against all these the apostle strenuously set himself (1 Cor. vii. 10–24).

His one advice was, "Stay as you are." If a believer is married to an unbeliever, so long as the latter is willing to abide in the marriage tie let it be carefully and honorably maintained. Whatever was done, the home life must be watchfully guarded, for the sake of each and of the children. Let not the Christian Jew be eager to cast aside all the religious restraints and sacred associations of the old Hebrew religion, and let not the Gentile convert be in a hurry to adopt the rites and usages of the Old Testament ritual, since it was waxing old and was ready to vanish away. Let not the slave adopt any revolutionary methods to become free, nor plot for the overthrow of the system of society which laid so heavy a yoke on him and his class. Each was urged to abide in the calling in which he was called. There are lessons here for us all.

As to the Home Life.—Very often the ties of the home life seem very irksome to young people. They fret at the duties they have to perform, the hours they have to keep, the arbitrary restraint to which they have to submit. Then they get restless and want to get away, or they become taciturn and sullen, shutting themselves up as far as possible in a shell. In some towns in England there is a growing tendency on the part of young people to leave their parents' home and take lodgings for themselves. This is a serious mistake. It is not fair to those who have sacrificed much for long years when no return was possible, and it evades the blessed discipline of the home life, which is of priceless value to us all.

What the angel of God said to Hagar I would repeat to all those who are meditating escape from uncongenial conditions: "Return and submit," even though dispositions chafe and irritate and the bit hurts the tender mouth. Of course there may be cases in which God has clearly shown that it is His will for the stern discipline to cease, and has opened a door of escape. In that case the apostle tells us by all means to use it (21); but if the door is not open we are not to force it; if the yoke is not broken we are not to shirk it. When God says, "Go forth free," we have no hesitation in obeying, but we must always distrust the dictates of our own choice and caprice.

How knowest thou that thou hast not been placed in that home to save the children, to win the younger brothers and sisters for God, to turn the heart of some disobedient one to the wisdom of the just? Stay there, then, till God says your work is done and you are at liberty to go elsewhere to be a vessel for His holy use.

AS TO THE CHURCH LIFE.—On the whole it is best to remain in the church in which we received our earliest religious impressions. It is, speaking generally, detrimental to the best interests of the religious life to be perpetually shifting, seeking new pastures, and running from one church to another. We may sometimes have to go forth as a protest, or we may be driven out; but in such cases our course is generally clear and unmistakable if we seek to act as the glory of Christ and the interests of His kingdom demand.

As to our Spheres of Daily Life.—
"Brethren, let each man, wherein he was called, therein abide with God." We often hear of "the call" to the ministry, or a woman's vocation to be a nurse, and attach a sacred significance to the words. But we speak more lightly of a man's "calling" and hardly realize how much meaning underlies the phrase. Let each of us believe that our daily business is the result of a divine call. The call may have come through the choice of a parent, the prompting of our own desire, a newspaper advertisement, or what may seem chance; but behind it and through it lay the choice and call of God. Dare to believe this, and that you are in the direct line of obedience when you come to the duties that ring out their summons as each day returns.

Called by God to be a physician or a surgeon; called to make chairs or boots; called to be a domestic servant or a laborer; called to be a merchant or a mechanic. He who called Isaiah to be a prophet has called thee, and all that thou hast to do is to abide in

Him, to count on His companionship and fellowship, to do all as beneath His eye and for His approval, and while doing the most trivial duties to be each day growing sweeter, stronger, nobler.

The other day I saw some novices taking lessons in bicycling. They went round and round the same track, but at each circuit they were improving in their knowledge and use of their machines. So in common life we may have to do the same thing with monotonous repetition, but in the meanwhile we may be growing in grace and the knowledge of God. If God opens the door to something else, of course use it; but if not, do not fret or chafe. Even if others pass thee, keep quiet and humble and go on preparing thyself for thy great opportunity; and when it suddenly comes to thee, as it came to Joseph, thou wilt be prepared by thy behavior in the prison to pass to the palace with its larger opportunities.

XXII

WHAT HAVE YOU TO GIVE?

"Silver and gold have I none; but such as I have give I thee."—ACTS III. 6.

THERE was a great contrast between the Gate Beautiful, standing on the top of the flight of fifteen steps that led from the lower terraces of the temple to the sacred level of the holy shrine, and the helpless beggar that lay at its foot. It towered far above his prostrate form, composed of the finest metal of the world, while he lived upon the scant gifts of charity; it needed twenty men to roll its exquisitely carved leaves backward and forward, while friends as poor as himself daily carried to the same spot his wasted form. Such a contrast obtains still between the beautiful gates of nature's temple, the beautiful gates of song and art and music, the beautiful gates of dawn and eve and childhood, as contrasted with the misery that sin has brought on those who lie broken and helpless on the steps trodden by the world's life.

But there was a greater contrast still between the appearance of the two apostles, as they climbed those steps at the hour of afternoon prayer, and the resources concealed beneath their humble guise. To the eye of the world they were but two poor peasants; before the gaze of God's angels they stood possessed of a secret which would unlock the measureless stores of eternity.

When first they stood against him, bidding him look on them, he thought that they would give him alms. Quaint Andrew Bonar suggests that he may have somehow heard of the recent distribution among the members of that early church and have thought that he was now to receive a share. If so he must have been disappointed to learn that, though so much had passed through the hands of its foremost leaders, not one coin had stuck to the lining of their pockets, and it was news to him that penniless men had something to give that could not be counted up in coins of precious metal. "Silver and gold have I none; but *such as I have* give I thee."

What comfort is suggested by these words to some of us, who have neither the silvery tongue of eloquence nor the golden ore of knowledge, who, like Moses or Jeremiah, cry, "Behold, I am a child; I cannot speak!" Believe me, young people, that gold and silver are the last things that men need.

They can dispense with these more quickly than with the gifts of the heart; and though you have none of them, either literally or symbolically, though you have nothing to distinguish you in the way of talent or gift, though you may account yourself unable to supply the lack that cries aloud from the heart of your fellows, yet you may have and give that which silver could not purchase and gold could not procure, and compared with which the rubies of the mine would be worthless as bags of pebbles.

Remember that the world has been enriched more through the poverty of its saints than by the wealth of its millionaires. Remember that the men whose hymns and words and achievements are the priceless heritage of the ages—that the martyrs, confessors, reformers, prophets, teachers, and leaders of men—have all been classed in that great and noble brotherhood which Peter represented when he became the medium through which the wealth of paradise passed into the common coinage of earth. These men have given blood, tears, spiritual impulses, faith, hope, love. What have you to give?

What did Peter include in the expression "such as I have"? You may be sure he did not refer to his vehemence, petulance, or cowardice—to those outbreaks of his own idiosyncrasy which had marred the happy years of relationship with his Lord; these would have been a sorry gift indeed. Better not to live than to pass on such an inheritance. But he must have referred to the blessed gifts which had come to hand through the grace of his risen Lord. Had He not gone up on high and received gifts for men, even for the rebellious? Had He not received of the Father the supreme gift of the Holy Ghost? Had He not, and only recently, shed Him forth in a golden shower of blessing? Had not the tongue of fire settled on Peter's head and the gift of a new courage filled his soul? Was he not conscious of a faith in the name of Christ through which lame men might be made whole, of a love which would bear and endure all things for Christ's sake, of a hope in the times of refreshing which must surely come again to a parched and dying world? These things he had, and he knew he had them, and he knew that he could give them also. The Son of God had come and given him an understanding and a power, a realizing sense of the Unseen and an unction from the Holy One. Rich in these sacred gifts, he felt that he might be a spendthrift in their distribution; dowered as God's heir, he could imitate the generosity of God, who giveth to all men liberally, and upbraideth not.

WHAT HAVE YOU TO GIVE? 145

Have you anything like this? Is there aught in your heart with which to enrich this poor and needy world? All around the beggars lie, with their whining voices, their thin outstretched hands, their helplessness and misery. Are you preparing to go into the great temple of life by yourselves, passing alone through the beautiful gate of early manhood and womanhood? or will you pick up the lame beggars as you pass by, lifting them up and leading them in with you, your joy being doubled by theirs, and your praises being all the sweeter because you hear them praising God and saying, as they hold you tightly, " Oh, magnify the Lord with me, and let us exalt His name together "?

What have you, young maidens, with which to enrich and bless the world? See to it that you seek and obtain from the risen Christ something which all the culture of these modern days can never give—the modest purity, the patient love, the encouragement of an invincible hope. Beauty in art or dress or face cannot heal the gaping wounds of men. If these be all they will lie at the Beautiful Gate unhelped. But Christ will give you that which, while it costs you nothing to receive, will make the lame leap as a hart and the tongue of the dumb sing.

What have you, young men? See to it that in Jesus Christ you get that purity, that manly strength, that authority to cast out devils, that power in prayer, which are characteristic of the highest life possible to men. You may get gold as the years pass, but this will not make you more able to bless men than you are to-day, when as yet you own nothing of the wealth of the world. Poor, you may make many rich if you have found the pearl of great price and by faith have learned to avail yourself of the unsearchable stores treasured in the divine Redeemer.

Passing through the Vatican on one occasion, Thomas Aquinas came on the pope superintending the counting of a great donation. "See," said the pope, "the church has left behind the days in which she said, 'Silver and gold have I none.'" "True, holy father," was the reply; "but can she say to the lame, 'Rise and walk'?" See to it, young friends, that growing wealth does not rob you of the divine and blessed power of meeting the needs of souls that money cannot touch.

XXIII

THE PRESENCE OF GOD

"He dwelleth with you, and shall be in you."—
JOHN XIV. 17.

THE constant realization of the presence of God has frequently been referred to by men of holy living as one of the most important rules in sanctification. It includes everything. If we could once acquire the habit of living in the sense of the immediate nearness of God, it would restrain us from evil more effectually than it is said the presence of a little child will do, and it will prompt us to all that would be well pleasing in His sight. But it was easier for those to recognize it habitually who were undistracted by the perpetual rush of modern life than for us, at the doors of whose senses so many impressions and appeals are constantly knocking. And it can only be acquired by careful attention to the temper of our soul. It is our present purpose to show how this habit may be formed.

In the early morning, as soon as you awake to consciousness, remember that you are in the very presence-chamber of God, who has been watching beside you through the long dark hours. Look up into His face and thank Him. Consecrate to Him those first few moments before you leave your couch. Look on toward the coming day through the golden haze of the light that streams from the angel of His presence. You can forecast very largely what your difficulties are likely to be, the quarters from which you may be attacked, the burdens that may need carrying. Take care not to view any of these apart from God. Be sure that He will be between you and them, as the ship is between the traveler and the ocean, be it fair or stormy.

As you gird yourself for the day, putting articles of clothing upon your person, remember that God supplies you with vesture clean and white, with the meekness and gentleness of Christ, with the garments of salvation, the robes of righteousness, and the jewels of Christian virtue. Do not look at these things apart from Him, but remember that they are attributes and graces of His own nature with which to array yourself. And above all put on the armor of light, remembering that God is light. You are to put on Christ, who is God manifest in the flesh, and you are to descend from your room into the arena of daily battle as one who is endued with the beauty of His character. This concentration of thought upon God during the act of dressing will prepare the soul for those acts of adoration, thanksgiving, and intercession which arise to God as the fragrant incense of the temple.

Amid the pressure of daily life trust the Holy Spirit, who is emphatically the divine Remembrancer, to bring all things to your remembrance and to recall you to the equipoise of your consciousness of God. There is no duty in life, however trivial and commonplace, that may not be dignified by being rendered to God as our bounden duty and service. This is, indeed, the secret of lifting all life to a noble and happy elevation. To do all for the Lord Jesus, to see Him standing behind every human relationship, to do the meanest and most irksome things because He takes them as service rendered to Himself, for which He will give a reward—this is Christian life, this makes the presence of God real, this dignifies the sweeping of a room.

"My mother asked me to turn the mangle for her, and I didn't want to," said a girl the other day; "but I thought Jesus was standing against it, saying, 'Do it for Me!' and I was glad; it seemed beautiful to do it for Him."

Your master may be gruff, irritable, and hard to please, but be sure that in obeying and pleasing him as far as conscience admits you are serving the Lord Christ. Thus every incident in daily life gives an opportunity of practising the presence of God.

Equally in our hours of recreation we may set the Lord always before us. Remember that it is said of the elders of Israel that they saw Jehovah, and there was under His feet as it were the paved work of a sapphire stone; they beheld God, and did eat and drink. How many eat and drink without beholding God! How many whose consciences were uneasy might behold God without daring to eat and drink! Happiest are they who are so at rest in Him that they do not hesitate to perform the natural functions of life with perfect ease, though all the while they recognize that He is nearer than hands or feet, nearer than breathing. The sense of God's presence would check immodesty, levity, self-indulgence, excess in eating or drinking, while it would give a new zest to all that was natural and innocent.

> " Heaven above is softer blue,
>   Earth around is sweeter green,
> Something lives in every hue
>   Christless eyes have never seen.
>
> "Birds with gladder songs o'erflow,
>   Flowers with deeper beauties shine,
> Since I know, as *now* I know,
>   I am His, and He is mine."

Often we have entered a room which we had thought to be filled with strangers. The gathering has presented no special attractions to us in the anticipation. Suddenly through the crowd we have beheld the face of one we love—the center of the central group, admired, his least word eagerly listened to, his every movement followed. Immediately the room has become filled with that one presence. All fear is dispelled; every object glistens with a new light; there is a charm which neither art nor music could yield. You have the sense that your presence is to him what his is to you. Such is the difference that comes to the soul when it has learned the practice of the presence of God.

One prime means of realizing the presence of God is to recognize that everything beautiful in anything, that everything lovely in any one, that any radiant gift dropped suddenly into our life, is due to Him—a beam from the Father of light, a flower cast from His hand on our path, the glint of His smile. It is a blessed habit to look steadfastly away from the things that annoy and irritate, in the circumstances and persons around us, to the traits that are pleasing and attractive. Dwell on these; count that in everything and every one there is something that God can love. Find this out. Look up to God and thank Him for it. And thus the beautiful and good will be a ladder of gold to climb into His presence. Often a box of flowers coming into my room has startled trifling thoughts from the feeding-grounds of earth to take flight with the rustle of wings into the blue sky, which is the tabernacle of the Most High.

Similarly bitter and disagreeable things may help us to remember God. Just because they are so hard to be borne, just because nothing but an infinite love could have permitted them to come in order to make us partakers of His blessedness, just because they cast so dark a shadow on our lives, we are compelled the more to recognize that God is near. I suppose God never seems so near as in dark days, when we can only live a moment at a time, when the stealthy tread of the nurse is the only sound in the curtained room, when the scenes in which we had played so conspicuous a part have faded, and we have lost our interest in them, and we look out on the ocean that laps against the wall of the room in which we lie. God, God, God only! Our heart cries with a great longing for God—as the hart for the water-brooks, as the babe for its mother, as the watcher for the dawn.

It is a frequent complaint that the spirit of reverence is leaving the world. Listen to a number of tourists admiring the Alps.

What adjectives! what exclamations! what a litter of provisions, the paper strewing the delicate beauty of the crystal snow and the glacier's blue depths! Note the majority of travelers entering some ancient cathedral or church, much more eager to study points of architecture, decoration, or restoration than to allow the spirit of worship to settle down with its mysterious spell. Too often our religious services lack in dignity, the sense of the infinite, and sink to the level of a performance or play. All this arises from the deficiency we have been complaining of. All would be altered if once we knew, with the knowledge of the deepest conviction, that we lived and moved and had our being in God.

How well I remember when first I visited Switzerland that my bedroom window, perched in Les Avants, looked across the blue of the Lake of Geneva toward that noble line of snow-capped mountains that border its southern shore. It seemed, for the brief fortnight that I lived there, as though the spell of that mighty vision held me enthralled. I slept and awoke and wrote and conversed as one on whom a new dignity had fallen. Could I ever be mean or selfish in the presence of that mystery of purity and solemnity? This and much more shall be the temper of the soul which, by the grace of the Holy Spirit, has learned habitually to recognize and cultivate the presence of God as revealed in Jesus Christ our Lord.

It is the special prerogative of the Holy Spirit to impart this to loving and believing souls. He loves to make Jesus real, to bring all things to our remembrance, to open blind eyes.

www.ingramcontent.com/pod-product-compliance
Lightning Source LLC
Chambersburg PA
CBHW070447090426
42735CB00012B/2482